Palgrave Studies in Practice: Global Fashion Brand Management

Series Editors

Byoungho Ellie Jin, Wilson College of Textiles, North Carolina State University, Raleigh, NC, USA
Elena Cedrola, Department of Economics and Law, University of Macerata, Macerata, Italy

Branding and internationalization are critical aspects of any business, and the fashion industry is especially global in nature. Very few apparel items are entirely produced within one country, and it is relatively easier for fashion brands to enter international markets because little financial investment is required, small-scale retail space is possible, and economies of scale can be maximized. Accordingly, there are more successful internationalization cases in the fashion industry than any other sector, yet no one text handles these critical topics (i.e., branding and internationalization) in one book, particularly in case study format. This series will focus on fashion brand cases that have been successful in global marketplaces. By examining their strategies in diverse aspects such as internationalization, innovation, branding and communication, and retail management, these books will help students, scholars, and practitioners grasp lesser-known yet effective international marketing strategies.

Eirini Bazaki · Vanissa Wanick
Editors

Reinventing Fashion Retailing

Digitalising, Gamifying, Entrepreneuring

palgrave
macmillan

Editors
Eirini Bazaki
Winchester School of Art
University of Southampton
Southampton, UK

Vanissa Wanick
Winchester School of Art
University of Southampton
Southampton, UK

ISSN 2523-3505 ISSN 2523-3513 (electronic)
Palgrave Studies in Practice: Global Fashion Brand Management
ISBN 978-3-031-11184-6 ISBN 978-3-031-11185-3 (eBook)
https://doi.org/10.1007/978-3-031-11185-3

This Palgrave Macmillan imprint is published by the registered company Springer Nature Switzerland AG
The registered company address is: Gewerbestrasse 11, 6330 Cham, Switzerland

Foreword

Fashion retailing is rapidly changing, due to the continuous progress of technology that constantly provides new supporting tools, and consumers' changing needs and demand of new experiences. Also, new challenges emerged strongly for the industry. For instance, the emerging need of more sustainable manufacturing processes and materials largely affects the industry, requiring changes to the traditional business models while limiting the impact on the environment and climate change. Similarly, fashion retailing is required to better promote inclusivity and diversity, being accused to not always properly understand diverse age, gender, sexuality, age, size, religion and individual's abilities. In other words, fashion does not often show how it might appeal to someone with, for instance, limited use of arms or with prosthetic.

COVID-19 pandemic further accelerated the decline of many brands, many fashion brands suffered lockdowns, stores closure, consumers' habits change and the request of new retail models to maintain the revenue while offering new safe and efficient shopping experience. For instance, in the UK the Trinity Group (A chine-owned upmarket fashion agglomerate including Gieves & Hawkes and Cerruti) went into administration, as well as Victoria's Secret UK, Brooks Brothers UK Division; while ASOS (the UK online fashion retailer) has acquired TopShop, Topman and Miss Selfridge (which shut down all the stores after the takeover, including the flagship one in central London, now acquired by

IKEA), Debenhams (the oldest retail chain in the UK) went into liquidation, closing down its stores forever, and T M Lewin (shirt and ties brands) has been acquired becoming on online brand only.

Thus, also fashion retailing needs to evolve and reinvent itself! This book offers a fresh and comprehensive perspective on the huge role played by new technologies, with emphasis on advanced recommender systems, social media, augmented reality and "metaverse", and on the important role of game and gamification experiences to promote brands.

The subject of *entrepreneuring* is a further interesting topic that makes the book compelling reading. Specifically, the book presents the case of Chiara Ferragni, how the influencer started from the blog "The Blonde Salad" in Italy to become an international fashion influencer and an entrepreneur with her own fashion brand; and the opportunities of crowdfunding to be meaningful for consumers in the new competitive scenario.

This book is an excellent contribution to contemporary inquiry in fashion retailing that brings together theoretical discussion with practice, supported by empirical research and case studies.

Eleonora Pantano, Ph.D.
School of Management
University of Bristol
Bristol, UK

Eleonora Pantano, Ph.D. is Senior Lecturer in Marketing. Her research activities mainly relate to the development of new customer solutions and retail management strategies, with emphasis on the role of new technology, artificial intelligence and machine learning algorithms.

Her findings appear in several books and textbooks, and in international peer-reviewed journals (i.e., *Annals of Tourism Research, British Journal of Management, Journal of Business Research, Psychology and Marketing*). Her papers have also consistently pushed the frontiers in the area of marketing and have become highly cited by academics in the field.

Contents

Notes on Contributors

Dr. Bazaki Eirini is Author, Lecturer and Researcher in Digital Marketing and Brand Management at Winchester School of Art, University of Southampton. Eirini is a graduate of Saïd Business School, University of Oxford, a Fellow of the UK Higher Education Academy, holds a Ph.D. in Marketing from Adam Smith Business School, University of Glasgow, an MSc in Management Research from the University of Glasgow, an M.Sc. Degree in Marketing Management from Aston University and a B.Sc. (Hons.) in Sociology from the Department of Social Sciences, Panteion University. Eirini research interests lie in fashion marketing, luxury marketing, branding and e-retailing. Her research work is published in leading academic books and international journals and has previously been presented at the 2021 Global Fashion Marketing Conference, 2019 Academy for Design Innovation Management Conference UK, the European Academy of Marketing Conference and Athens Institute for Education and Research. Eirini actively advises fashion and luxury brands on how to build a strong brand identity, connect with customers and drive sales through digital channels.

Dr. Buckingham Christopher is award-winning Teacher who lectures on research methodologies and methods. His main role as Senior Lecturer at Winchester School of Art (University of Southampton) is teaching on the Global Advertising & Branding (M.A.). He also helped to create the undergraduate programme Business of Games and helps on various business modules within the creative industries.

Chris' background is in crowdfunding. He is an entrepreneur, an investor, a mentor and an author who has taught at several UK and European universities.

Cedrola Elena, Ph.D. is Dean of the Department of Economics and Law at the University of Macerata (Italy). In the same University, she is Full Professor and teaches management and international marketing. She was Visiting Scholar at the Beijing Normal University (China), at the Paris IV Sorbonne University (France) and at the Aix-Marseille University (France). Dr. Cedrola's research areas are international management and marketing for small and medium-sized enterprises. She has an extensive portfolio of intellectual contributions comprising of refereed journal publications, presentations, invited keynote speeches, lectures and workshops. Her latest studies focus on country of origin in the industrial sectors.

de Barros Costa Evandro is Professor at Federal University of Alagoas, Brazil. He received a B.Sc. degree in Computer Science from Federal University of Paraiba (UFPB), Brazil in 1988, an M.Sc. and a Ph.D. degree in Electrical Engineering from UFPB in 1989 and 1997. His research interests include knowledge representation and reasoning, personalised recommendation systems, machine learning and multiagent systems.

Landim André R. D. is an M.S. student at Federal University of Campina Grande (UFCG), Brazil. He is Software Engineer at UFCG. His research focuses on Artificial Intelligence.

Moura J. Antão B. got his Ph.D. in Electrical Engineering from the University of Waterloo, Canada in 1982. Antão is currently Professor of Computer Science at the Federal University of Campina Grande (UFCG), Brazil. Over the years, he has worked extensively on modelling and performance evaluation of computer networks. More recently, he has been researching IT economics and its applications to business-driven IT management particularly of (fashion) e/m-commerce scenarios.

Pereira Artur M. is a Ph.D. student at the Federal University of Campina Grande (UFCG), Brazil. He holds a Master's degree in Computer Science from Federal University of Alagoas (UFAL), Brazil. Currently, he is Application Developer at IBM Brazil. His research interests are Machine

Learning, Personalised Recommender Systems, Deep Learning, Natural Language Processing, and Knowledge Representation.

Dr. Reay Emma is a video game scholar whose research is located at the intersection of childhood studies, education research and aesthetic criticism. Her interests include constructions of childhood in digital spaces, cuteness and affect in contemporary games, and justice and equity in the games industry. She is Lecturer in Media and Communications Studies at Anglia Ruskin University and teaches Game Design at the University of Southampton.

Dr. Stallwood James is Senior Teaching Fellow at the University of Southampton, teaching courses of mathematics and programming for the University's Games Design and Art degree. His research interests are behavioural AI modelling, with recent publications in adaptive emotive modelling for machine learning.

Vieira Thales is Professor at the Institute of Computing, Federal University of Alagoas (UFAL), Maceió, Brazil. He holds a Ph.D. degree in Mathematics from Pontifical Catholic University of Rio de Janeiro (PUC-Rio) in 2010. His current research interests include Machine Learning, Computer Vision, Natural Language Processing and Pattern Recognition.

Dr. Wanick Vanissa is Senior Lecturer at the Department of Art & Media Technology at Winchester School of Art, University of Southampton. She currently teaches at the B.A. Games Design & Art programme. Vanissa holds a Ph.D. in Design from the University of Southampton, UK, M.B.A. in Marketing from University Federal Fluminense (UFF), Brazil and a BA in Design at PUC-Rio, Rio de Janeiro, Brazil. She is also Fellow of the Higher Education Academy (FHEA). Her research interests are multidisciplinary and include cross-cultural Human-Computer Interaction (HCI), games design methodologies, creativity and diversity, inclusive extended reality (XR), storytelling and culture, games for social good and well-being and sustainable consumer behaviour across cultures.

List of Figures

Chapter 1

Chapter 2

Chapter 3

Chapter 4

Chapter 5

Chapter 6

Chapter 7

List of Tables

CHAPTER 1

The State of Fashion Retailing Post-pandemic: Trends, Challenges and Innovations

Vanissa Wanick and Eirini Bazaki

Abstract Fashion is one of retailing's most actively reshaping, transforming and reinventing itself sectors. This introductory chapter offers a theoretical foundation towards online retail trends, challenges and innovations in the fashion industry in a post-pandemic world. It also provides contextual background towards the 'reinvention' of fashion retailing, by illustrating how customers and brand relationships and strategies have changed. Considering this, the chapter has analyzed relevant literature, provides recent market examples from the pandemic and post-pandemic

V. Wanick (✉) · E. Bazaki
Winchester School of Art, University of Southampton, Southampton, UK
e-mail: vwv1n12@soton.ac.uk; v.w.vieira@soton.ac.uk

E. Bazaki
e-mail: e.bazaki@soton.ac.uk

E. Bazaki and V. Wanick (eds.), *Reinventing Fashion Retailing*, Palgrave Studies in Practice: Global Fashion Brand Management ,
https://doi.org/10.1007/978-3-031-11185-3_1

era. Main themes that emerged from the literature review include (1) digitalization of fashion retailing; (2) gamification and playfulness; (3) entrepreneurship and blogging; (4) customer-driven and tech-savvy business models.

Keywords Fashion retailing · Trends · Challenges and innovations · Entrepreneurship · Gamification and playfulness

1 Introduction

Digitalization is reshaping and rapidly transforming the fashion retail industry (Nixdorf, 2022). Since the beginning of the pandemic, purchases across social media channels have increased 68% worldwide (Statista, 2021a). The pandemic has forced brands to innovate and adopt digital transformations in a rapid pace. In 2020, the luxury goods market saw a decrease on value from 281 billon EUROS (in 2019) to 217 billion EUROS (in 2020). But the market has managed to recover and in 2021 its value was 283 billion, even higher than the pre-pandemic period (Statista, 2021b). The pandemic has boosted consumer digital engagement and new shopping habits were incorporated. According to McKinsey & Company (2021), 48% of consumers moved to online shopping due to the pandemic.

Fashion brands are already exploring a future where boutiques are no longer the only place to shop. This is impacting the way shoppers can contribute to creatively shop at home, such as, using mobile apps and virtual try-ons powered by Augmented Reality (AR) technologies.

Alongside these developments, it is important to ensure customer satisfaction and requirements. The integration of smart technologies with service design and applications introducing the virtual fitting room are on the increase and are contributing to the fierce competition between online retailers. However, there is little understanding about the most effective way to use this technology and how it can transform services touchpoints, particularly for fashion brands.

Another aspect to consider is how to integrate the fashion e-commerce experience with Artificial intelligence (AI). Trends in the e-retailing industry show that AI can provide a more personalized experience to consumers, due to AI algorithms and machine learning (ML) processes that can not only recommend the best clothing to consumers but also interact with them promoting a more interactive scenario.

With the need for a more convenient and real-time experience, technologies have been used to address consumer needs and to respond to abrupt changes in consumer behavior. This chapter seeks to answer three research questions:

1. What are the drivers of the digital transformation in fashion retailing?
2. How can brands become more digital savvy? What tech innovations and challenges lie ahead?
3. What are the implications of this digital transformation in terms of connecting and communicating with consumers across multiple channels?

A conceptual framework closes the chapter with the keywords to the answers that will be further discussed in the following chapters.

2 Responding to Change: The Need for Reinvention

According to McKinsey & Company (2021), ten themes emerged after the pandemic and require attention from fashion retailers; these are represented by categories such as:

- Global economy impacts (mostly represented by uneven recovery and logistics disruptions);
- Changes in consumer behavior (moving towards domestic luxuries, wardrobe 'reboot' and the 'metaverse mindset', boosted by engagement of young consumers);
- Fashion systems (social shopping, circular textiles, authentication, cyber resilience and changes in recruitment);

Luxury brands are also hoping to reinvent themselves and attract young consumers. One example is the integration of non-fungible tokens (NFTs) for the authentication of digital garments and the quest to conquer the 'metaverse' (Joy et al., 2022). This trend can become an opportunity for companies to explore ways towards community building and creativity, which can go beyond the 'physicality' of the garments. Virtual clothing is becoming a big deal for fashion brands, where NFTs can be used as authentication tools and collectables (McKinsey & Company, 2021).

A process of digital consumerism is emerging from the constant collaboration between brands, games and virtual worlds. Games, for example, are no longer a space solely driven by entertainment. Brands are constantly engaging and collaborating with game worlds. *Vans*, *Gucci* and *Ralph Lauren*, for instance, have collaborated with *Roblox*, an online game platform that hosts user-generated game creations. Luxury brands might want to explore fashion events through live stream platforms, which are also on the rise and have become more mainstream since the pandemic (Rathi et al., 2022).

3 Digitalization

Digitalization that started well before the COVID era and rapidly accelerated since then rendered fashion retail, faster, more diverse and also more easily adaptable than other industries (Otto, 2022). Many processes have been turned upside down; omni-or multi-channel e-commerce has paved the way for the biggest technological revolution in fashion retail history (Otto, 2022). Although there is still work to be done, major trends such as VR, social commerce and gaming adopted by tech-savvy brands and consumers show the continued willingness and readiness of fashion retail players.

Digital innovations can also be used in-store and are not limited to e-commerce. For instance, digital signage and displays can be used in-store and have a positive effect on consumer behavior, since it influences both cognitive and emotional responses from consumers (Kim et al., 2020). However, this influence might differ according to the brand category. Kim et al. (2020) found that this effect was higher in sport stores if compared to other fashion luxury stores. This shows that there is a difference across brand categories when it comes to digitalization and consumer behavior.

Social media platforms have been used to build relationships with consumers, with a significant increase of preferences towards video and images instead of text such as Instagram (Mazzucchelli et al., 2021). Although these platforms sound promising, there is also a potential for fashion brands to increase their presence in international markets through the social media channels, such as by using the *Facebook* buy button

(Mazzucchelli et al., 2021). In fact, in 2022, *Facebook* is still the most used platform worldwide with nearly 3-million users, followed by *YouTube* and *WhatsApp* (Statista, 2022). This shows that social shopping is on the rise. This is crucial because marketing through social media is the most popular channel for luxury marketing (Rathi et al., 2022).

Coupled with that, the COVID-19 pandemic has forced fashion retailers to adapt and innovate. This has shifted retailing strategies towards a more digital approach, which included the adoption of VR/AR and 3D technologies. This brings new challenges and opportunities for retailers to connect with consumers and keep them engaged. One strategy is through gamification. Gamification is the use of game design elements in non-gaming contexts (Deterding et al., 2011), mostly applied as psychological and motivational strategies (Almarshedi et al., 2016). In fact, gamified elements such as goal setting, achievement and avatar customization can be employed in order to evoke more motivational effects to consumers (Lau & Ki, 2021). In this particular study, Lau and Ki (2021) utilized the app *Taobao life*, a 3D application that allows consumers to try outfits virtually through their avatar. Avatar customization had a significant impact on consumers' motivational effects since it triggered a sense of autonomy (Lau & Ki, 2021). This shows that for digital fashion, the avatar has a crucial role to play. Taobao life is not the only application in the market. For instance, in 2021, *Ralph Lauren* partnered with *Bitmoji*, a tool for users to build their own avatars via Snapchat. In this case, consumers can purchase the items from the brand's website. *Bitmoji* is a virtual avatar, with the same properties and features of an emoji, but with the user's customized attributes. Users can create their own avatars and use them in different channels, not just in platforms such as *Snapchat*. *Bitmoji* can be used in games and in different 'lenses' through the users' phone camera via Augmented Reality (AR); the 3D version was just launched in 2021.

Another aspect to consider is the role of human avatars in the Virtual Fitting Room (VFR). On one side, it discusses issues such as the development of avatars and virtual fittings for consumers to better understand whether a product fit (Muta et al., 2018; Polke & Kumari, 2018). In fact, by cross-referencing data from virtual and physical try-ons, Artificial Intelligence (AI) algorithms, based on Back Propagation Artificial Neural Networks (BP-ANNs) can be used to improve garment fit through predictive analytics (Liu et al., 2022).

With the online fashion industry projected to grow by 26% to nearly $1tr (753 bn) in market worth until 2025 (Nixdorf, 2022), fashion brands seek to offer a seamless online shopping experience, tailoring in-app purchase journeys, virtual fitting rooms and livestreaming. Fashion brand corporations such as *Nike*, *Gucci*, *Louis Vuitton* and *Balenciaga* have dived into the metaverse to rip the opportunities of this emerging market. Nike has teamed up with Roblox to build its own virtual world called *Nikeland*, and has also acquired metaverse fashion brand RTFKT that uses 'cutting edge innovation to deliver next-generation collectables that merge culture and gaming' (Nixdorf, 2022), Balenciaga took on open-world video game, *Fortnite* where players could purchase digital outfits inspired by real-life Balenciaga pieces. Some items like Balenciaga's Triple S Sneakers could also be unlocked, while the hub was live for one week and only for players to interact to tie this up with the real-world Balenciaga made a series of clothing available in selected Balenciaga stores and the website (Gibson, 2022).

4 Gamification, Virtual Worlds and the 'Metaverse'

Digital consumerism is blossoming and it has been reflected by the emergence of the 'metaverse' (Joy et al., 2022). For instance, a *Gucci* virtual handbag has been sold for more than $3000 USD in *Roblox* in 2021 (Clayton, 2021). *Roblox* is a community-driven space, in which people can build virtual worlds and play games. *Ralph Lauren* also joined *Gucci* in the *Roblox* landscape, through a holiday thematic experience that lasted nearly a month (the case is discussed in Chapter 3).

The 'metaverse' provides a blend between physical and digital worlds, in which the avatar plays a central role. The definitions of 'virtual worlds' and 'metaverse' might overlap; according to Nevelsteen (2018), the 'metaverse' allows real-time interaction, whereas virtual worlds do not. At times the concepts get also confused, as virtual worlds are not necessarily games; however, they might have elements from games, such as avatars. Although this idea might sound as a fad, the concept of merging physical and digital experiences has been explored by luxury brands through the combination of mobile and ubiquitous media in service design, with the rise of concepts like Luxury 4.0 and 'phygical' luxury experiences (Lawry, 2022, p. 2).

It is important to mention, though, that fashion and games do not have an initial relationship based on consumerism; in fact, fashion in games can be represented via dressing-up activities and identity expression (Makryniotis, 2018). In addition, fashion in games can impact the game-play (Makryniotis, 2018), as for instance, a player could wear a garment that allows power-ups and role-playing attributes (Kim et al., 2012). Thus, critical questions might arise from the emergent use of games and immersive technologies by luxury fashion brands. Do we want to replicate the same power relations and consumerism to the digital world? What role does fashion play on consumer well-being via digital garments and avatar dressing-up activities? Considering that games and virtual worlds provide opportunities for participation and community-driven creativity, what power do consumers have in this scenario?

Avatars are digital representations of ourselves and the way they are represented might influence one's negotiation skills (Yee, 2007). Thus, since fashion extends the concept of the self (Loussaïef et al., 2019), the way the avatar is portrayed not only expands the idea of the self but it also aids on self-representation and expression. This means that the avatar itself together with digital fashion choices can have a double 'layer' of self-expression: one via the choice of avatar (e.g., skin, hair, type body, etc.) and the other via digital garments.

The landscape of game design and fashion skills is also changing. 3D simulation systems of dynamic garments and animations can be expanded across both areas (Choi, 2022). The digital world provides affordances and materialisms that might be more difficult to achieve in the physical world, such as animated garments and shape-shifting clothing. Thus, another trend to consider is the application of fashion skills to gaming and vice-versa.

Coupled with these digital trends, there is also the rise of digital fashion companies. Mentioned by Joy et al. (2022), *Dress X* is a start-up company that solely creates and sells digital garments. This opens possibilities for new services to emerge. In this particular case, *Dress X* sells the idea that being digital is also sustainable. The company also offers a space for 3D designers to collaborate and reproduce their work.

Gamification can also be used to provide brand co-creation and participation, through rewards, challenges, a sense of community, social interaction and customization, as for instance, when playing a game, consumers might feel they are part of the brand (Nobre & Ferreira, 2017). Additionally, gamification can be employed in VFRs by providing consumers the opportunity to customize and create their own 3D avatars (Lee & Xu, 2020). Gamification of the shopping process can also be experienced through social connections, by commenting on each other's outfits (Lee & Xu, 2020). In fact, luxury brands can also benefit from gamification and games through storytelling (Lawry, 2022). Games are also platforms for storytelling. World building is also another skill that brands need to master, if they are willing to connect with consumers in virtual worlds (Hackl, 2020).

The pandemic has boosted the need for social connections and community building both in digital and in physical worlds (Chitrakorn, 2021). Due to lockdown and constant social isolation needs, games emerged as a coping mechanism. *Animal Crossing New Horizons (AC:NH)* was the most popular and more downloaded game during the pandemic and helped families to cope with a collective problem (Pearce et al., 2021). Chapter 5, in fact, talks about video games and brands and uses *AC:NH* as one of the case studies. For instance, the luxury brand *Net-a-Porter* collaborated with *AC:NH* and developed a 'world' packed with player activities and social events. Thus, games not only allowed players to encounter a safe space during the pandemic, but also provided new spaces for people and brands to co-create.

5 Entrepreneurship

The proliferation of the use of social media in recent years, has changed the way business works and interacts with customers. With US consumers spending an average of two and a half hours daily on social media in 2021 (Nance, 2021), social media have become an integral part of consumer's lifestyle. Consumers rely on social media sites for information, communication, participation and purchasing. Nance (2021) in her work on entrepreneurship through the use of social media, highlights the emergence of the blogger-turned entrepreneur phenomenon. The growth of e-commerce, social commerce and mobile apps, combined with the rise of the fast-fashion have eased and increased consumption of fashion garments. Fashion conscious consumers are left in seek of authentic insight knowledge to facilitate their choices, which has in turn led to the proliferation of fashion interested individuals who capitalized on the opportunities for interaction offered by social media to share their fashion opinions, offer advice, make comments and recommendation. Fashion bloggers who often start with a personal blog and manage to increase their influence through the use of social media and e-WOM, at a later stage partner with brands to monetize their blog, increase their insight and influence while offering brands the opportunity to grow their customer base with loyal fashion followers led by the fashion blogger. Most research on personal blogs focuses on the influencer's motivations, characteristics and behaviors (Choi, 2020; Delisle & Parmentier 2016; Lee & Xu 2022; Mainolfi & Vergura, 2022). Few studies focus on fashion bloggers as entrepreneurs (Gustafsson & Khan, 2017; Nance, 2021; Xie et al., 2021) and investigate the entrepreneurial aspects of fashion blogging. The current study in line with Nance (2021), we define entrepreneurs as fashion bloggers who have turned their personal blog into a successful business, have built a personal brand and launched other freestanding business that started as a result of blogging. An in-depth case study of Chiara Ferragni, renowned fashion blogger entrepreneur in Chapter 6 and relevant academic literature is used to uncover the key activities, behaviors and attributes of a successful fashion blogger entrepreneur (Nance, 2021).

Social media's proliferation among consumers has made market entry more accessible allowing ordinary consumers to gain market share as self-employed entrepreneurs as well as small business owners. A popular way to achieve this is through creating, maintaining, monetizing and growing a blog. Bloggers with their ability to enter and prevail in established markets have redefined what it means to be a business owner. Bloggers have made such a significant impact on their audiences' tastes, styles and purchasing habits that have managed to shift a once business-driven market to a consumer-driven one (Nance, 2021).

Bloggers have become such powerful intermediaries that even well-established fashion brands with a long history and tradition include them in their marketing. This phenomenon of a blogger-turned entrepreneur is mostly seen in the last couple of years. Famous bloggers-turned entrepreneurs include Ree Drummond TV presenter of the Food Network show, Pioneer Woman, features on the cover of People magazine, owns a houseware brand, a restaurant and a hotel. Ree Drummond started her career personal blog 'The Pioneer Woman' in 2006. Another notable example is that of Chiara Ferragini, famous blogger, entrepreneur who started in 2009 with a personal blog 'The Blonde Salad' and has built an empire of her namesake brand 'The Chiara Ferragni Collection' sits at the board of famous Italian luxury brand Tod's and is also 100% owner of the TBS Crew Ltd, the company that manages the online lifestyle magazine of her formal personal blog 'The Blonde Salad'.

Entrepreneurship comes in many forms (Nance, 2021) and there are many definitions of the term in the literature. Based on the study at hand, an entrepreneur is defined as a creative, innovative, risk-taking person who is capable of identifying opportunities in its external environment, use resources in the best way to exploit these opportunities (Cuomo et al., 2017). The current study on the blogger-turned entrepreneur will analyze the personality traits and characteristics, the key resources and strategies that contribute to this duality. Another theory that one can say interrelates with entrepreneurship theory and has a strong explanatory power of this phenomenon is the leadership theory. Fashion leadership, opinion leadership, taste leadership all describe a set of criteria that define the success of the fashion blogger-turned entrepreneur phenomenon. Another aspect that is discussed in Chapter 6 is the strategy of authenticity and its various applications and interpretations in the context of social media and the blogosphere. While authenticity is a popular buzzword in today's consumer-driven market, there is little and even conflicting evidence of its true meaning and existence. Some recent literature also looks at specific authenticity strategies beyond self-representation and reflects different aspects of authenticity (Audrezet et al., 2020). With reference to specific case studies, this book seeks to better understand the multi-dimensionality and application of this concept.

6 Conclusion and Other Chapters

This chapter addressed the trends and challenges of fashion retailing in a post-pandemic world, which can be summarised in Fig. 1. By looking at examples and research conducted from 2019 onwards, this chapter identified three key strands and themes that underline the narrative of this book:

1. Digitalization: impacted by AI algorithms and recommendation systems applied to e-commerce (this theme is addressed in Chapter 2); digital atmospherics and the influence of emergent media in fashion retailing such as mobile AR applications and VFR (this is addressed in Chapter 4)

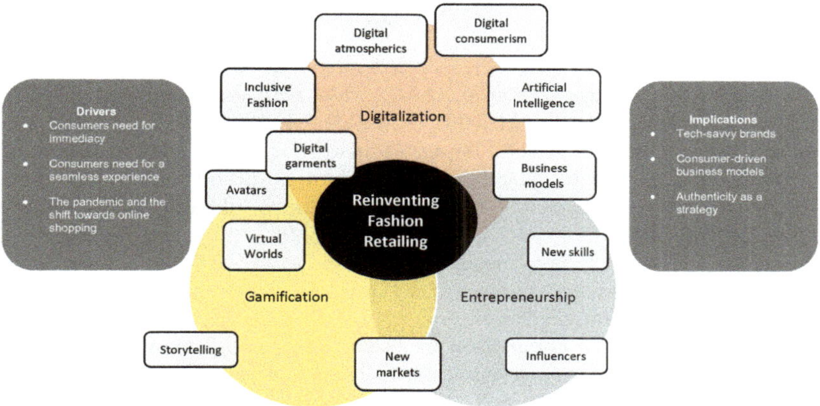

Fig. 1 The international online fashion retailing environment trends, drivers and implications (*Source* Developed by the authors)

2. Entrepreneurship: mostly looking at the blogger-turned entrepreneur phenomenon, social commerce, person-branding and leadership theories (this theme is addressed in Chapter 6)
3. Gamification: mostly boosted by the use of avatars and world-building spaces, gamification is a relationship between game design elements and fashion branding components and be implemented via virtual worlds, game economies and systems and social interactions (these topics are addressed in Chapters 3 and 5)

Intersections between each theme are also discussed. For instance, digital garments and avatar design can be both applied in digitalization and gamification; business models can be discussed between digitalization and entrepreneurship; new skills can be discussed via the intersection between gamification and entrepreneurship.

References

Almarshedi, A., Wanick, V., Wills, G., & Ranchhod, A. (2016). Gamification and behaviour. In Stieglitz et al. (Eds.), *More than just games* (pp. 19–29). Springer. https://doi.org/10.1007/978-3-319-45557-0_2

Audrezet, A., de Kerviler, G., & Guidry Moulard, J. (2020). Authenticity under threat: When social media influencers need to go beyond self-presentation. *Journal of Business Research, 117*, 557–569. https://doi.org/10.1016/j.jbusres.2018.07.008

Chitrakorn, K. (2021). *How brands can tap the future of social | Vogue Business*. https://www.voguebusiness.com/companies/the-future-of-social-is-multiplayer-what-fashion-needs-to-know

Choi, A. (2020). Social comparison in fashion blogging: "creative self" as the new genre in fashion communication. *Journal of Fashion Marketing and Management, 24*(4), 651–665. https://doi.org/10.1108/JFMM-07-2019-0140

Choi, K. H. (2022). 3D dynamic fashion design development using digital technology and its potential in online platforms. *Fashion and Textiles, 9*(1), 1–28. https://doi.org/10.1186/S40691-021-00286-1/TABLES/3

Clayton, N. (2021). *Someone spent over $4,000 on this Gucci bag in Roblox | PC Gamer*. https://www.pcgamer.com/uk/someone-spent-over-dollar4000-on-this-gucci-bag-in-roblox/

Cuomo, M. T. et al. (2017). Enablers for end-user entrepreneurship: An investigation on Italian food bloggers. *Psychology and Marketing*, *34*(12), 1109–1118. https://doi.org/10.1002/mar.21051

Delisle, M. P., & Parmentier, M. A. (2016). Navigating person-branding in the fashion blogosphere. *Journal of Global Fashion Marketing*, *7*(3), 211–224. https://doi.org/10.1080/20932685.2016.1167619

Deterding, S., Dixon, D., Khaled, R., & Nacke, L. (2011). From game design elements to gamefulness. In *Proceedings of the 15th International Academic MindTrek Conference on Envisioning Future Media Environments - MindTrek '11*, 9. https://doi.org/10.1145/2181037.2181040

Gibson, D. (2022). *5 Brands already boldly embracing the metaverse. The Drum*. https://www.thedrum.com/news/2022/01/17/5-brands-already-boldly-embracing-the-metaverse

Gustafsson, V., & Khan, M. S. (2017). Monetising blogs: Enterprising behaviour, co-creation of opportunities and social media entrepreneurship. *Journal of Business Venturing Insights*, *7*, 26–31.

Hackl, C. (2020). *Social VR, Facebook Horizon and the future of social media marketing*. https://www.forbes.com/sites/cathyhackl/2020/08/30/social-vr-facebook-horizon--the-future-of-social-media-marketing/?sh=425375e65b19

Joy, A., Zhu, Y., Peña, C., & Brouard, M. (2022). Digital future of luxury brands: Metaverse, digital fashion, and non-fungible tokens. *Strategic Change, 31*(3), 337–343. https://doi.org/10.1002/JSC.2502

Kim, S. J., Kim, K. H., & Mattila, P. (2012). The role of fashion in the characters of online games. *Journal of Global Fashion Marketing, 3*(2), 81–88. https://doi.org/10.1080/20932685.2012.10593110

Kim, H. Y., Lee, Y., Cho, E., & Jung, Y. J. (2020). Digital atmosphere of fashion retail stores. *Fashion and Textiles, 7*(1), 1–17. https://doi.org/10.1186/S40691-020-00217-6/TABLES/4

Lau, O., & Ki, C. W. C. (2021). Can consumers' gamified, personalized, and engaging experiences with VR fashion apps increase in-app purchase intention by fulfilling needs? *Fashion and Textiles, 8*(1), 1–22. https://doi.org/10.1186/S40691-021-00270-9/TABLES/5

Lawry, C. A. (2022). Futurizing luxury: An activity-centric model of phygital luxury experiences. *Journal of Fashion Marketing and Management: An International Journal* (ahead-of-print). https://doi.org/10.1108/JFMM-05-2021-0125

Lee, H., & Xu, Y. (2020). Classification of virtual fitting room technologies in the fashion industry: From the perspective of consumer experience. *International Journal of Fashion Design, Technology and Education, 13*(1), 1–10. https://doi.org/10.1080/17543266.2019.1657505

Lee, H., & Xu, Y. (2022). Influence of motivational orientations on consumers' adoption of virtual fitting rooms (VFRs): Moderating effects of fashion leadership and technology visibility. *International Journal of Fashion Design, Technology and Education*, *0*(0), 1–11. https://doi.org/10.1080/17543266.2022.2048423

Liu, K., Wu, H., Zhu, C., Wang, J., Zeng, X., Tao, X., & Bruniaux, P. (2022). An evaluation of garment fit to improve customer body fit of fashion design clothing. *International Journal of Advanced Manufacturing Technology*. https://doi.org/10.1007/s00170-022-08965-z

Loussaïef, L., Ulrich, I., & Damay, C. (2019). How does access to luxury fashion challenge self-identity? Exploring women's practices of joint and non-ownership. *Journal of Business Research, 102*, 263–272. https://doi.org/10.1016/J.JBUSRES.2019.02.020

Mainolfi, G., & Vergura, D. T. (2022). The influence of fashion blogger credibility, engagement and homophily on intentions to buy and e-WOM: Results of a binational study. *Journal of Fashion Marketing and Management*, *26*(3), 473–494. https://doi.org/10.1108/JFMM-03-2020-0050

Makryniotis, T. (2018). Fashion and costume design in electronic entertainment—Bridging the gap between character and fashion design. *Fashion Practice, 10*(1), 99–118. https://doi.org/10.1080/17569370.2017.1412595

Mazzucchelli, A., Chierici, R., Di Gregorio, A., & Chiacchierini, C. (2021). Is Facebook an effective tool to access foreign markets? Evidence from international export performance of fashion firms. *Journal of Management and Governance, 25*(4), 1107–1144. https://doi.org/10.1007/S10997-021-09572-Y

McKinsey & Company. (2021). *State of Fashion | McKinsey*. https://www.mckinsey.com/industries/retail/our-insights/state-of-fashion

Muta, M., Ishikawa, Y., Yamanaka, T., & Masuko, S. (2018). Oz's fitting room: Fashion coordination support system by digital signage and human-driven virtual agent. In *Proceedings of the 7th ACM International Symposium on Pervasive Displays* (pp. 1–2). https://doi.org/10.1145/3205873.3210711

Nance, D. R. (2021). *Entrepreneurship through the use of social media: An exploration of the blogger-turned-entrepreneur phenomenon in the fashion industry*. https://repository.lib.ncsu.edu/handle/1840.20/38490/Dissertation/North/Carolina/State/University.US

Nevelsteen, K. J. L. (2018). Virtual world, defined from a technological perspective and applied to video games, mixed reality, and the Metaverse. *Computer Animation and Virtual Worlds, 29*(1), e1752. https://doi.org/10.1002/cav.1752

Nixdorf, D. (2022). *The two most important trends influencing fashion retail. Retail Week*. https://www.retail-week.com/retailvoice/the-two-most-important-trends-influencing-fashion-retail/7041456.article?authent=1

Nobre, H., & Ferreira, A. (2017). Gamification as a platform for brand co-creation experiences. *Journal of Brand Management, 24*(4), 349–361. https://doi.org/10.1057/S41262-017-0055-3/TABLES/3

Otto, A. (2022). *Fashion retail 2022—three trends, three predictions*. Retrieved October 21, 2022, from https://fashionunited.com/news/retail/fashion-retail-2022-three-trends-three-predictions/2022022145954

Pearce, K. E., Yip, J. C., Lee, J. H., Martinez, J. J., Windleharth, T. W., Bhattacharya, A., & Li, Q. (2021). Families playing animal crossing together: Coping with video games during the COVID-19 pandemic. *Games and Culture*, 155541202110561. https://doi.org/10.1177/15554120211056125

Polke, N., & Kumari, S. (2018). Avatar manager system for online fashion clothing APP. In *2018 International Conference on Information, Communication, Engineering and Technology, ICICET 2018, August*, 1–4. https://doi.org/10.1109/ICICET.2018.8533812

Rathi, R., Garg, R., Kataria, A., & Chhikara, R. (2022). Evolution of luxury marketing landscape: A bibliometric analysis and future directions. *Journal of Brand Management, 29*(3), 241–257. https://doi.org/10.1057/S41262-022-00273-X/FIGURES/5

Statista. (2021a). *Change in social commerce usage by region 2021a | Statista*. https://www.statista.com/statistics/1276422/change-social-commerce-usage-worldwide-region/

Statista. (2021b). *Value of the global luxury goods market 2021b | Statista*. https://www.statista.com/statistics/266503/value-of-the-personal-luxury-goods-market-worldwide/

Statista. (2022). *Most used social media 2021 | Statista*. https://www.statista.com/statistics/272014/global-social-networks-ranked-by-number-of-users/

Xie, Q. et al. (2021). The influence of entrepreneurial characteristics on the performance of tourism vlogger entrepreneurs. *Frontiers in Psychology*, *12*(August), 1–12. https://doi.org/10.3389/fpsyg.2021.725545

Yee, N. (2007). The proteus effect: Behavioral modification via transformations of digital self-representation. In *PhD Dissertation* (Issue June). http://www.nickyee.com/pubs/Dissertation_Nick_Yee.pdf

CHAPTER 2

Helping Online Fashion Customers Help Themselves: Personalised Recommender Systems

Artur M. Pereira, Evandro de Barros Costa, Thales Vieira, André R. D. Landim, and J. Antão B. Moura

Abstract The massive size of fashion items catalogues, jointly with the explosive number of product combinations and specific customer preferences and traits—in what is known as the information overload problem—tend to degrade customers' online experience. To mitigate the effects of this problem and to improve customers' online experience, Recommender Systems (RSs) have been proposed. This chapter

---

A. M. Pereira (✉)
IBM Brazil, Hortolandia, Brazil
e-mail: artur.maia.pereira@ing.com

ING Netherlands, Amsterdam, The Netherlands

E. de Barros Costa · T. Vieira
Institute of Computing, Federal University of Alagoas, Maceió, Brazil
e-mail: evandro@ic.ufal.br

T. Vieira
e-mail: thales@ic.ufal.br

E. Bazaki and V. Wanick (eds.), *Reinventing Fashion Retailing*, Palgrave Studies in Practice: Global Fashion Brand Management ,
https://doi.org/10.1007/978-3-031-11185-3_2

provides an overview of Artificial Intelligence techniques for personalised RSs in online fashion retail stores. An introductory description of RSs is provided, including their components, potential applications, current commercial availability and limitations, and possible evolutionary avenues. Customer Models (CMs) are described and highlighted as a key component that allows RSs to provide personalised recommendations. The chapter also briefly explores how CM/RS combinations may assist stakeholders in fashion industry domains other than sales. Contents are intended as a primer for the seasoned or apprentice fashion professional in academia or industry to realise Fashion CM/RSs' potential to facilitate fashion online sales or to transition the fashion industry from product-centric to customer-centric operations. Real-world examples illustrate the main concepts; complementary reading sources are provided.

Keywords Fashion · Recommender system · Customer model · Online shopping · E/M-commerce

1 Introduction

Fashion online shopping should reach almost 40% of the total sales of the fashion industry in 2022.[1] Scaling up sales staff to assist customers with their online shopping through voice/video calls or text chat is not the best option: too costly and slow. Letting shoppers consider, by themselves, the many choices in large online catalogues of fashion items may lead to cognitive and choice overloads (Sweller, 1988) and consequently

---

A. R. D. Landim
Computer Science Graduate Program, Federal University of Campina Grande (UFCG), Campina Grande, Brazil
e-mail: andredantas@copin.ufcg.edu.br

J. A. B. Moura
Systems and Computing Department, Federal University of Campina Grande (UFCG), Campina Grande, Brazil
e-mail: antao@computacao.ufcg.edu.br

[1] www.marketingcharts.com/industries/retail-and-e-commerce-106623

disappointing online shopping experiences. As fashion online retailing[2] grows, alternatives to efficiently and effectively help customers decide what to buy are required. Fortunately, this can be accomplished through Artificial Intelligence (AI) algorithms to recommend items that match customers' preferences and needs.

In a nutshell, a fashion recommender system (RS) tries to reproduce recommendations of fashion items that a salesperson would make to a prospective customer. In other words, a RS aims to be a digital version of a fashion sales assistant.

An effective RS is crucial for successfully conducting an e-commerce business in general and fashion in particular (An et al., 2019). Making adequate, personalised fashion recommendations is a complex task. It is dependent on many short- and long-term factors, such as occasion, purchase history, individual preferences, interpersonal influences, age, gender, physical characteristics, season, culture, availability of items, and experience (learning). Fortunately, AI's methods, algorithms, and tools may come to the rescue. AI RSs are being increasingly deployed by major e-commerce platforms—e.g., Amazon, eBay, and specialised fashion sites—e.g., Zara, Farfetch.

An effective AI-based fashion RS processes information acquired from the customer (through a suitable interface); and, from databases with the fashion items catalogue, the model for the customer's profile, behaviour and preferences, and knowledge on fashion styling to produce recommendations and, possibly, associated explanations also.

This chapter takes you on a tour of a typical AI RS for fashion e/m-commerce, illustrating main concepts and components, their interdependencies, input, and output (Sect. 2) through examples of real-life fashion sites and a simple RS for a small apparel store (Sect. 3). The evolution and applications of RSs to other domains of the Fashion Supply Retail Chain (FSRC) are also explored (Sect. 4), besides e/m-commerce. Suggestions of complementary reading (Sect. 5) and cited references are also provided.

[2] The term "online retail(ing)" is used here to refer to any form of Business to Consumer (B2C) selling fashion products or services over the Internet. It encompasses the modalities of e-, m- (mobile-), s- (social network-), c- (collaborative-), and t- (television-) commerce. "Online shopping" or "e-commerce" may be used interchangeably here for any of these modalities unless otherwise stated.

The chapter is intended to facilitate fashion practitioners—in academia or the industry—to understand, adopt, and explore RSs for online fashion retailing.

2 An Overview of Fashion Recommender Systems

RSs are techniques and software tools that help consumers to access online product catalogues, gather data about their interests and tastes, and suggest product items that may interest them. The basic idea is to recommend products of interest among extensive existing options. For personalised recommendations, by using data filtering tools, the system must consider individual consumer preferences, needs, contexts, and other collected data. This section presents the main approaches of RSs that have been used in several areas, including fashion; it then emphasises knowledge-based recommenders that explicitly use a customer model (CM) to represent knowledge on the customer. Finally, some comments related to fashion online shopping are offered.

2.1 Main Approaches in RS

RSs follow different approaches—of which there are three main ones: content-based filtering, collaborative filtering, and hybrid filtering (Ricci et al., 2015).

Content-based filtering recommendation techniques use characteristics about products to suggest items related to the ones the customer has liked or browsed in the past, based on information about item-to-item comparisons present in the preference history of this consumer (Bobadilla et al., 2012). Such is the case when a RS suggests ties that go well with a formal dressing after a customer previously liked or browsed some tuxedos.

Collaborative filtering is the most common technique for recommendation and represents customer preference based on the similarity of customers or items from the interaction data. It relies on the assumption that if a group of customers rates a class of items similarly, or if they share a similar consumer behaviour, they will probably share the same preferences (Goldberg et al., 2001). For instance, a customer browsing running shoes may receive a recommendation for running socks because people that bought the shoes also bought the socks.

Knowledge-based recommenders suggest items to customers based on domain knowledge about how items meet customer preferences and needs. In general, they, implicitly or explicitly, rely on three types of knowledge: about the customers, the product items, and recommendation criteria—the matching of an item to the customer's needs (Adomavicius & Tuzhilin, 2005).

CMs for RSs may be static when only long-term preferences are considered; dynamic, when both long-term and short-term preferences are represented. Identifying a customer's short-term and long-term preferences is a relevant concern. For instance, a customer from a tropical country may frequently browse and purchase summer outfits (long-term); the customer may also visit a store to occasionally buy a winter coat for a vacation trip (short-term). For a comprehensive review on RSs, we refer the reader to (Bobadilla et al., 2013).

2.2 RSs Based on Customer Models

These RSs include an implicitly or explicitly represented CM to support personalised recommendations. The CM represents information about an individual customer or group that is essential for a RS to provide the personalisation effect.

The general structure of the RS is shown in Fig. 1, highlighting a conceptual framework containing components, such as a user (fashion customer in the case here) interface (or "UI" for short), inference engines, knowledge base (KB), item fashion database. This RS works as follows: the customer queries the RS, providing data/facts about the situation. Then, the Recommendation Engine (RE) compares data of the situation to the KB, then gives a recommendation or asks for more information if needed.

2.2.1 RS Main Components

As Fig. 1 illustrates, the RS processes information acquired from the customer (through a customer interface) and databases. These databases may comprise the fashion items catalogue; the model for the customer's profile, behaviour, and preferences; knowledge on fashion styling. The acquired information is used to produce recommendations and associated explanations.

The customer interface includes question–answer facilities, sometimes allowing (written or spoken) dialogue in natural language—using chatbot technology, say. The RE is responsible for inferring and recommending

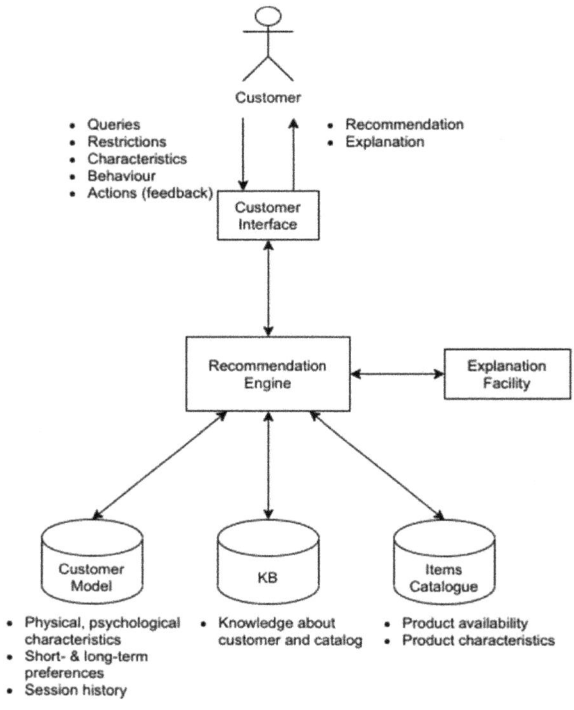

Fig. 1 Conceptual Framework of a knowledge-based RS with explicit CM (*Source* the authors)

items that may interest the customer. The KB stores all relevant information used by the RS, including knowledge about customers' characteristics and fashion items. The CM may contain both concrete observations and data, including a customer context, and inferred knowledge about the customer as an internal representation of him/her. The Explanation Facility allows a customer to understand how the RE arrived at certain conclusions or results. That is, it explains *how* the RS arrived at a particular recommendation. The Catalogue contains descriptions of items associated with each fashion category, including information such as images, size, colour, forms.

2.2.2 *A Remark on RS Components' Achievement*

Discussing ways to achieve the functionality and integration of the RSs' components of Fig. 1 is beyond the scope of this chapter. Suffice to remark that many options are available to developers—e.g., information for building and updating a CM may be gathered online or offline, using chatbots, inferences about shoppers' behaviours or choices, or collecting data with questionnaires—as illustrated in Sect. 3.

2.3 *Applicability to *-Commerce*

The above conceptual discussion of FRSs applies to any online retail modality in Footnote 2. Differences are mainly technical and arise in the interface component of Fig. 1. Whereas the term "e-commerce" was meant to cover all modalities, the letter prefix of the newer terms points to the type of device or setting that supports the UI. For instance, in m-commerce, the buying and selling of goods happen through mobile devices.

Current implementation tools allow for automatic adjustments of an app's screens to the UI device in a transparent manner—e.g., screen size and format viewing (Marcotte, 2017). Rest thus assured: the understanding you acquired about FRSs in general from the conceptual discussion in this section will serve you well regardless of the fashion online retail modality you will be considering. Aspects of the UI device are not addressed in the discussion that follows.

3 Reality Check

This section illustrates the main concepts presented in this chapter. We describe an FRS experience and the exposition of real-world cases.

3.1 *Recommending a Single Clothing Item*

We introduce a simple experience with an FRS developed for research purposes and deployed for a small fashion store by our team. The system learns personalised customer preferences through its interactions and recommends catalogue items accordingly. The customer is supposed to be unknown to the system at first. The recommendation process consists of two major steps.

First, given a clothing category (skirt, dress, etc.) chosen by the customer, a set of items is sampled from the catalogue to build an initial gallery. Since we do not have any prior fine-grained information about the customer except the clothing category, the initial gallery is built following a partially random strategy that tries to maximise fashion item features diversity, thus mitigating the cold start problem.

Next, the customer interacts with the gallery by providing explicit feedback on gallery items. More specifically, the customer may classify items' images to express whether he/she likes or dislikes them. Then, Machine Learning (ML) algorithms are employed to learn the customer's preferences from its feedback and update (or create) an individual CM. The updated CM is exploited to build a new smart gallery with new items from the catalogue while still trying to improve the diversity of the gallery. These last two steps run in a loop until the customer finds items that match its preferences. It is also worth mentioning that, from this second-generated gallery, two criteria are simultaneously considered: one exploits the CM to provide customised recommendations; the other is aimed at improving the diversity of items of the gallery, thus allowing the customer to explore the whole catalogue.

Figure 2 shows an illustrative example of our proposed FRS. Mary is going on vacation to a tropical beach and needs a new skirt. Mary knows that when she visits e-commerce sites for the first time, she is likely to receive general recommendations that might not satisfy her, such as new items, best-sellers, and deals. To get personalised recommendations, she initially gives feedback about some skirt samples following simple criteria: she likes (looking for) short skirts and dislikes long skirts. We used these two criteria in the simulation for simplicity. However, in a real-world scenario, the customer's feedback does not need to adopt any fixed attribute-based rule. We can see that the first gallery consists of a highly diverse selection of skirts. In particular, long skirt images are scattered along the three lines. As we move on in the iterative feedback-learning process, the following galleries are built through a threefold strategy: the first line shows skirts that Mary may like; the second line shows skirts that the ML algorithm is not sure if they match Mary's preferences; the third line shows skirts that Mary may or may not like.

This strategy is intended to avoid bias in the ML algorithm, which ideally should be fed with examples of both liked and disliked items, thus keeping a balanced set of labelled items. In addition, exhibiting skirts that the algorithm is not sure about Mary's preference may help it quickly

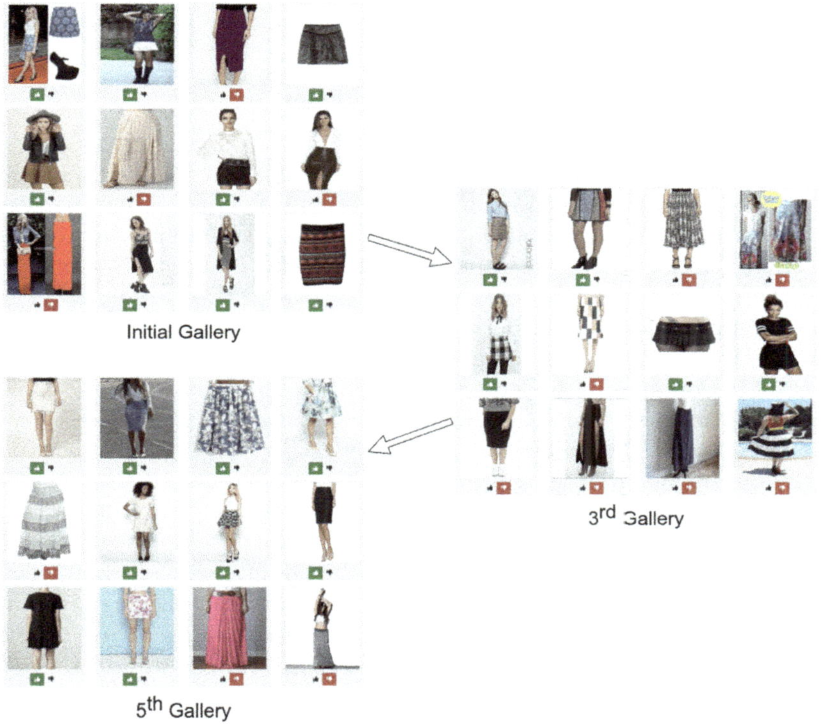

Fig. 2 Simulation carried out in our FRS, where the customer wishes for short skirts (*Source* the authors)

learn her preferences. In this specific simulation, one can see that the ML algorithm efficiently learnt Mary's preference: all skirts in the first line of the last gallery received likes. It is worth mentioning that Mary does not need to give feedback about all the gallery items. If an item is neutral for a customer, he/she could skip it. However, more feedback implies more data to teach the system, and consequently, that might result in better recommendations.

The images used in our prototype were harvested from the DeepFashion data set (Liu et al., 2016). We applied filters to eliminate redundancies, insufficient and inaccurate product feature classification; to restrict the experiments to a single clothing category, resulting in a data set with 13.300 skirt images. The data set is available in a public repository.[3]

3.2 Building a CM Through Questionnaire

Considering the full scope of the CM, the previously described system explicitly gathers information about a single branch of the CM: customer preferences about several product features. Using a different, simple, and yet effective approach, the solution proposed by Lookiero[4] (as of Q4-2021) applies a static questionnaire to compose a diversified CM. The questionnaire is divided into four categories regarding customer information: style, physical characteristics, intention, and profile. Figure 3 shows one of the questions for each category.

Going back to Mary's example, let's suppose she tried to buy her new skirt through Lookiero. She is supposed to answer the questionnaire at least one month before her trip because Lookiero does not offer a real-time service performed by an intelligent system. After answering Lookiero's questionnaire, a personal stylist (human) will analyse Mary's CM and periodically send a package to her home with recommended clothing and advice on how to combine them. Given a package of recommendations, Mary will only pay for items she wants to keep, returning the others without additional costs. Then, Lookiero will update Mary's CM based on the features of the clothing she bought and/or returned.

3.3 Recommending Fashion Items Combinations

CM / RSs are often based on implicit feedback, i.e., the CM is inferred from customer activities inside the e-commerce, such as views, purchases, or clicks. Farfetch.com, a retail store for luxury brands, offers (as of Q4-2021) two session-based and context-aware personalised experiences embedded into their e-commerce that considers the visual similarity of the items and complementary products.

The first one looks for visual patterns of items that the customer has clicked and tries to find similar items to recommend. Figure 4 shows an example of a recommendation based on visual similarity. After choosing

[3] https://github.com/ArturMaiaP/SkirtsDataset

[4] https://lookiero.co.uk/

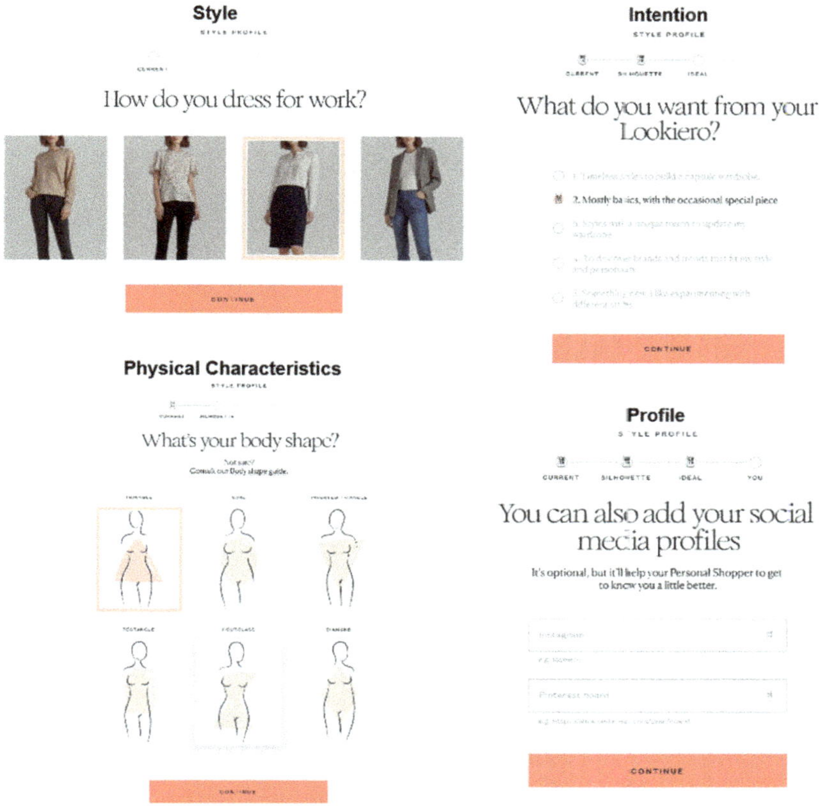

Fig. 3 Questionnaire applied to learn the CM (*Source* https://lookiero.co.uk/)

a skirt, Mary continues exploring e-commerce by herself, looking for a dress for a night party. When Mary clicked on a blue floral print dress, as no feedback was provided, the system inferred that she liked this dress and then suggested other blue dresses with similar print and form that she also may like.

In the second Farfetch.com approach, Mary first chooses an initial product, and then the RS automatically suggests complementary products to complete her outfit. This recommendation is based on thousands of predefined outfits manually created by the guidelines of Farfetch's sense

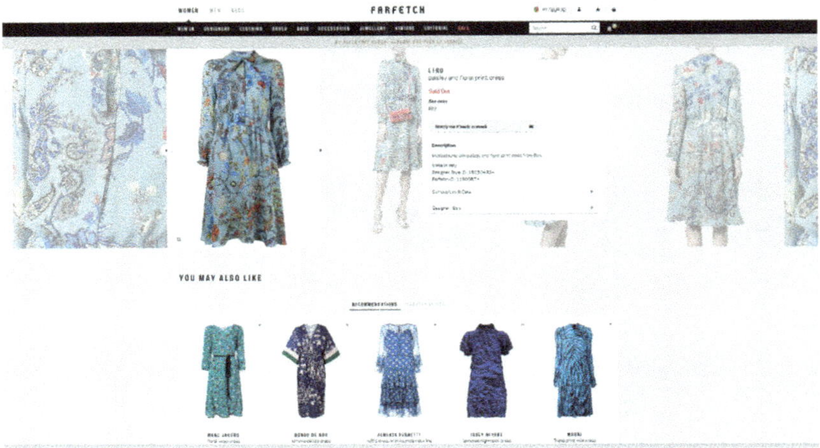

Fig. 4 Farfetch's recommendation by visual similarity to a dress initially selected by the consumer (*Source* https://www.farfetch.com/)

of style, validated by professional stylists. In Fig. 5, given the selected blouse, the system suggested an outfit composed of pants, earrings, shoes, and handbags. In this second approach, a product-centred model is used instead of a CM. However, since the initial product must be selected by the customer, we still consider that this approach implicitly provides a personalised recommendation.

4 Moving Forward

To a large extent, the quality of fashion shopping recommendations depends on the quality and comprehensiveness of the information the RS receives from the auxiliary components in the FRS structure of Fig. 1. The CM is likely the component that will offer better returns on investments to improve said quality. Moreover, major gains from enhancements of FRSs are likely to happen along two avenues: integration to virtual fitting rooms (VFRs) and other FSRC domains, besides online retail.

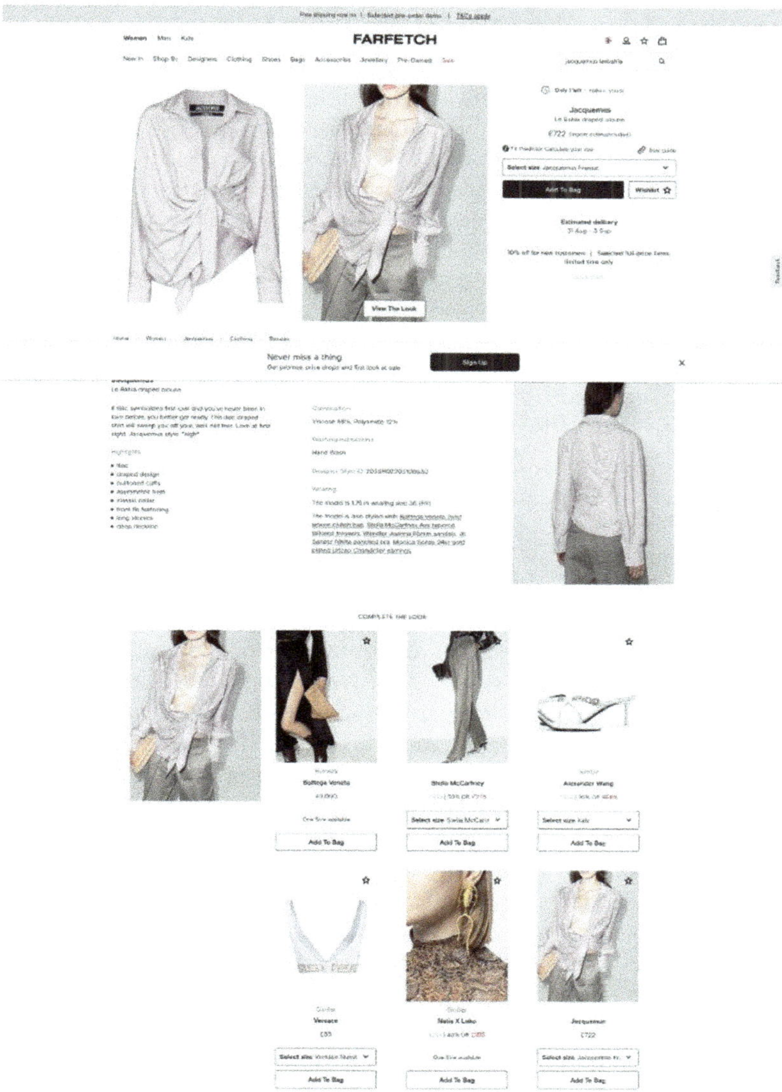

Fig. 5 Farfetch outfit recommendation from a blouse initially selected by the consumer. The system automatically suggests several products that go well with the blouse (*Source* https://www.farfetch.com/)

4.1 *Modelling Physical Features for VFRs*

One of the main challenges of fashion e/m-commerce is the impossibility to touch and try on before buying, which leads to uncertainty about the item, resulting in a higher return rate (Citrin et al., 2003). More returns, which may account for 20%–60% of fashion sales (Cullinane et al., 2019), imply higher operating costs and environmental concerns.

These problems may be mitigated by modelling the consumer's physical attributes and applying them to a VFR. Advancements in computer vision research are still needed, however, to achieve satisfactory quality, thus improving the consumer's experience, as exemplified by (Lee & Xu, 2020), which integrates a CM/RS to a VFR in a fashion e-commerce site.

4.2 *Integrating RSs into Other Online FSRC Domains*

Decisions are made in every domain of a FSRC: planning, production, logistics, retail (e/m-commerce), and returns. For instance, RSs may be used to support planning a new collection based on customers' profiles and behaviours stored in CMs or to produce products on demand. To improve warehousing and logistics, CM/RSs combinations could be used to better understand common preferences of customers in the same geolocation, facilitating product distribution by anticipating shipping, as discussed by Erevelles et al. (2016) and applied by Amazon in its Anticipatory Package Shipping patent (Spiegel et al., 2012).

Also, RSs may increase sales conversion rates (Mugge et al., 2010) by making recommendations using the information of modelled customers' behaviours during online retail. However, post-purchase behaviour plays an important role in replacement purchases or returns (reducing rates). Therefore, modelling customer-acquired product attachment information in the post-sales domain is important to provide better-informed recommendations.

The reader may glimpse how CM/RSs (or other AI solutions) are likely to be applied to other FSRC domains and the benefits this may bring to the fashion industry from the October 2021 interview of Levi Strauss' Chief Strategy Officer, Katia Walsh, for *The AI in Business* podcast (www.emerj.com).

5 Closing Remarks

This chapter presented an overview of AI-based RSs for fashion online retail. The conceptual nature of the presentation applies to any form of online retail modality—i.e., e/m/s/t-commerce, and the reader should be aware of the introductory purpose of the chapter's contents. Experimenting with the FRSs at fashion brand retail sites will help consolidate and deepen the insights the chapter may have given you on how FSRs may serve your organisation.

Additional sources of information you may want to check to complement or advance the FSR conceptual veneer the chapter offered include:

- Anderson and Coveyduc (2020) bring a roadmap for the adoption of AI technology and a discussion on which business problems are amenable to an AI treatment. Finding training data for AI systems and how to go about developing them for business value are also addressed. The focus is not on the fashion industry or RSs, but the book gives ideas for fashion applications.
- Dokoohaki (2020) and Dokoohaki et al. (2021) are collections of papers from academic and industrial research on RSs for retail, e-commerce, and fashion. They consider opinions from social media and fashion influencers, body size, first-time shoppers (cold start problem), and eventual returns to make recommendations of single fashion items or their combinations.
- Chakraborty et al. (2021) cover recent research results on ML, computer vision, and fashion retailing that explain the different FRSs and their inner workings in terms of process phases (learning and recommending), AI algorithms, and filtering techniques. The survey discusses metrics to evaluate the performance of FRSs. In particular, the authors explore image-based FRSs much in line with our discussion in subsection 4.1.
- Mueller and Massaron (2019) offer a glimpse from a beginner's vantage point on AI applications to online business and social media outlets. Notice, however, that parts of the book are meant for software developers.

References

Adomavicius, G., & Tuzhilin, A. (2005). Toward the next generation of recommender systems: A survey of the state-of-the-art and possible extensions. *IEEE TKED, 17*(6), 734–749. https://doi.org/10.1109/tkde.2005.99

An, H., Kwon, S., & Park, M. (2019). A case study on the recommendation services for customised fashion styles based on atificial intelligence. *Journal of the Korean Society of Clothing and Textiles, 43*(03), 349–360. https://doi.org/10.5850/jksct.2019.43.3.349

Anderson, J. L., & Coveyduc, J. L. (2020). *Artificial Intelligence for Business: A Roadmap for Getting Started with AI* (1st ed.). Wiley.

Bobadilla, J., Ortega, F., Hernando, A., & Bernal, J. (2012). A collaborative filtering approach to mitigate the new user cold start problem. *Knowledge-Based Systems (KBS), 26*, 225–238. https://doi.org/10.1016/j.knosys.2011.07.021

Bobadilla, J., Ortega, F., Hernando, A., & Gutiérrez, A. (2013). *Recommender Systems Survey. KBS, 46*, 109–132. https://doi.org/10.1016/j.knosys.2013.03.012

Citrin, A. V., Stem, D. E., Jr., Spangenberg, E. R., & Clark, M. J. (2003). Consumer need for tactile input: An internet retailing challenge. *Journal of Business Research, 56*(11), 915–922.

Chakraborty, S., Hoque, M. S., Rahman Jeem, N., Biswas, M. C., Bardhan, D., & Lobaton, E. (2021, July). Fashion recommendation systems, models and methods: A review. In *Informatics*, *8*(3), 49. MDPI.

Cullinane, S., Browne, M., Karlsson, E., & Wang, Y. (2019). Retail clothing returns: A review of key issues. *Contemporary operations and logistics*, 301–322.

Dokoohaki, N. (2020). *Fashion recommender systems (Lecture Notes in Social Networks)* (1st ed. 2020 ed.). Springer.

Dokoohaki, N., Jaradat, S., Pampín, H. J. C., & Shirvany, R. (2021). *Recommender systems in fashion and retail*. Springer Publishing.

Erevelles, S., Fukawa, N., & Swayne, L. (2016). Big Data consumer analytics and the transformation of marketing. *Journal of Business Research, 69*(2), 897–904.

Goldberg, K., Roeder, T., Gupta, D., & Perkins, C. (2001). Eigentaste: A constant time collaborative filtering algorithm. *Information Retrieval*, *4*(2), 133–151.

Lee, H., & Xu, Y. (2020). Classification of virtual fitting room technologies in the fashion industry: From the perspective of consumer experience. *International Journal of Fashion Design, Technology and Education, 13*(1), 1–10.

Liu, Z., Luo, P., Qiu, S., Wang, X., & Tang, X. (2016). Deepfashion: Powering robust clothes recognition and retrieval with rich annotations. In *Proceedings of the IEEE conference on computer vision and pattern recognition* (pp. 1096–1104).

Marcotte, E. (2017). *Responsive web design: A book apart n 4*. Editions Eyrolles.

Mueller, J. P., & Massaron, L. (2019). *Deep Learning For Dummies*. Wiley.

Mugge, R., Schifferstein, H. N., & Schoormans, J. P. (2010). Product attachment and satisfaction: understanding consumers' post-purchase behavior. *Journal of consumer Marketing*.

Ricci, F., Rokach, L., & Shapira, B. (2015). *Recommender Systems Handbook*. Springer Publishing.

Spiegel, J. R., McKenna, M. T., Lakshman, G. S., & Nordstrom, P. G. (2012). *U.S. Patent No. 8,271,398*. Washington, DC: U.S. Patent and Trademark Office.

Sweller, J. (1988). Cognitive load during problem solving: Effects on learning. *Cognitive Science*, *12*(2), 257–285.

CHAPTER 3

Brand Storytelling, Gamification and Social Media Marketing in the "Metaverse": A Case Study of *The Ralph Lauren Winter Escape*

Vanissa Wanick and James Stallwood

Abstract Since Facebook's rebrand to "Meta" in 2021, and the rise on collaborations between brands and consumers via User-Generated Content (UGC) platforms, brands are willing to win their own space in the "metaverse". This brings new challenges for fashion brands as social media marketers need to up their game and learn new skills such as world-building, collaboration and how to design playful experiences. This chapter provides an overview of the current debates about challenges in social media marketing in different UGC and social media platforms, through the lens of brand storytelling and media convergence. We start this chapter by reviewing the literature about brand storytelling and online communities, in order to identify storytelling elements that can be used by fashion brands across different types of social media. As a result, we have developed a conceptual framework to understand

V. Wanick (✉) · J. Stallwood
Winchester School of Art, University of Southampton, Southampton, UK
e-mail: vwv1n12@soton.ac.uk; v.w.vieira@soton.ac.uk

E. Bazaki and V. Wanick (eds.), *Reinventing Fashion Retailing*, Palgrave Studies in Practice: Global Fashion Brand Management ,
https://doi.org/10.1007/978-3-031-11185-3_3

how fashion brands can sustain a coherent story across different channels (including the metaverse). We have utilised this framework to undertake an analysis of *The Ralph Lauren Winter Escape*, which was hosted in the UGC platform *Roblox*, from 8th December 2021 to 3rd January 2022. Our findings show that the overarching story is sustained by the festive thematic and it is brand-centred; however, there was little connection with other social media platforms. Other insights show that rewarding mechanisms (e.g., gamification) and avatar customisation were used frequently to keep consumers engaged in the experience. Implications for both practice and theory are discussed, including the need for a more effective alignment of gamification strategies with emergent consumer narratives and the rules of the online community.

Keywords Social media · Marketing · Metaverse · Brand storytelling · Gamification · *Roblox* · *Ralph Lauren*

1 Introduction

The social media landscape is changing. In 2021, Facebook announced a rebrand for the name "Meta", which refers to the Greek word for "beyond", but also a short version for the term "metaverse". Simply put, in the "metaverse", people interact through avatars in virtual worlds. The concept is not new and has been utilised to define platforms such as Second Life (SL) in early 2000s and VRChat in 2015. The term metaverse has started as a science fiction idea, mostly set in dystopian worlds. Robertson and Peters (2021) published in website "The Verge" a summarised definition of the metaverse, as a term that should be equivalent to the Internet, and a virtual place that supports User-Generated Content (UGC), personalised avatars, 3D graphics and an overlap of digital and real-world activities, which can be game-related or not. Game scholar Ralph Koster (2021) distinguished the "metaverse" from virtual worlds, such as SL. Koster mentioned that SL is a world on its own, and that the metaverse is a combination of many worlds. The concepts, however, overlap. In this chapter, for sake of simplicity, we refer to the "metaverse" as virtual worlds: a place in which people can create worlds, communicate, interact, collaborate and (eventually) play games through avatars in 3D environments.

Research in the area of social media and fashion marketing has been advancing towards the amplification of the understanding about influencer marketing, brand-consumer relationships and online brand communities (Chu & Seock, 2020). However, although the brand message is the key, the platforms' features, the level of interactivity and the stories people tell in these platforms are also important. This means that the platform itself is not just what drives a successful campaign. Since people connect with stories (Woodside, 2010), it is imperative that brands connect with brand communities and fans to develop a compelling storyline (Smith & Wintrob, 2013). In social media channels, storytelling enables the transformation from an individual experience to a "relationship" experience, supported by brand communities, mostly through member's narratives (Pera & Viglia, 2016). This can be supported by UGC platforms. Social media allows consumers to engage with a brand via UGC such as reviews, videos, product photos, etc. (Smith et al., 2012). However, brand engagement via UGC can differ, according to the type of social media channel. For instance, *YouTube* features consumer's self-promotion, whereas *Twitter* is more centred around the brand (Smith et al., 2012). With the rise of marketing activities in virtual worlds/platforms such as *Roblox* and *Fortnite*, UGC in this space might also differ.

Roblox is a platform where people can play several games, most of them created by a community of players. *Roblox* can run in different types of devices, from computers to smartphones and it was launched in 2006. According to *The Guardian* (Dredge, 2019), in 2019, around 1.5 million children played Roblox in the UK; 40% of the global players are female. *Roblox* itself is not a game but a library of UGC made of games. The platform supports its own virtual currency (*Robux*) that can be used to buy items in the games, such as avatars and/or special weapons and abilities. Thus, making and collecting items can be a great business for *Roblox* content makers. Similarly, *Fortnite* (The Fortnite Team, 2020) allows players to experience special events and provides four game modes (one of them is a creative mode that enables players to design games and experiences in "islands"; however, the most popular mode is the Battle Royale [Roach, 2021]).

Spaces like *Roblox* and *Fortnite* have been attracting attention of brands. *Fortnite*, for instance, hosted a mega concert from *Ariana Grande* in August 2021, and, according to "The Verge", the experience fit the narrative of *Fortnite* itself (Webster, 2021). In 2021, luxury brand *Gucci* has partnered with *Roblox* and a famous content creator, to build the *Gucci Garden Experience* (Roblox, 2021). In this experience, visitors could immerse themselves into a flowery world and visitors' avatars could absorb patterns, colours and features from the environment, mimicking the *Gucci Garden Archetypes* exhibition from the real world. *Ralph Lauren* was also another luxury brand that partnered with *Roblox* in 2021 and will be studied as a case study in this chapter.

These partnerships set the scene for fashion brands willing to conquer a space in the "metaverse". However, questions arise. How genuine are these experiences? Are these experiences just a gimmick? *Forbes* has published two trendy articles addressing the future of social media marketing in the "metaverse". The first article (Hackl, 2020), addressed elements that should be part of the skillset of social media marketers, such as collaboration, playfulness and world-building. In November 2021, *Forbes* (Woo & Forbes Agency Council, 2021) recommended the need for brands to collaborate and co-create with consumers. This shows that just being part of these platforms is not enough. These virtual worlds are composed by vivid communities of different people who are constantly creating and sharing content; these worlds already have their underlining rules and brands need to understand them.

This chapter aims at providing a framework through an in-depth case study of the brand *Ralph Lauren* (RL) to outline the best practices to run a campaign across different social media platforms. The focus of this chapter is on the exploration of factors that enhance brand storytelling in virtual worlds. Concepts such as transmedia storytelling, gamification, audience participation and world-building also discussed.

The main exploratory research questions we aim at addressing in this chapter are:

- How do luxury fashion brands tell stories in different channels (e.g., social media and virtual worlds)?
- How much of these stories are generated by consumers and brand communities? Do they tell the same stories? How do they differ?
- Which factors affect brand storytelling across different channels (e.g., social media and virtual worlds)?

2 Theoretical Background

This section starts with an overview of research principles about social media marketing focused on fashion and luxury brands. This is followed by an in-depth analysis of storytelling principles, including virtual worlds, avatars and storytelling, brands storytelling and story types, storytelling across different types of media, storytelling and gamification, and storytelling in online brand communities, user-generated content and virtual worlds.

2.1 Social Media Marketing: Aligning Fashion Strategies with Self-Representation

Broadly speaking, social media marketing is originally brand-centric, but it can support the communication of the brand's values, vision and mission with several stakeholders, including the firms' employees (Felix et al., 2017). For luxury brands, social media marketing involves activities that build brand-consumer relationships, mostly through interactive media (Kim & Ko, 2012). In a study using the luxury brand Louis Vuitton (LV) as a prompt, Kim and Ko (2012) found five social media marketing activities of luxury brands that boost customer equity: entertainment (e.g., having fun with the brand), interaction (e.g., information sharing), trendiness (e.g., new/trendy fashion content), customisation (e.g., customised information) and word of mouth (e.g., willingness to share with others). Thus, experiences in virtual worlds could be a great landscape to achieve these five principles, since it provides a place for interaction that can be shared with others through graphical representations, such as avatars.

Fashion can evoke one's idea of self-concept and it extends the self by clothing and accessories (Loussaïef et al., 2019). For luxury brand consumers, identity is key. Adornments such as jewellery, can reinforce self-identity and enhance the "imagined" body, which can be seen as a "canvas" that can be layered with wearable art (Venkatesh et al., 2010). In this case, luxury fashion can be considered as art that one can wear, where the human body is just a "canvas", in which consumers can express their identity. Due to the idea of ownership, self-image and self-presentation, this sense of the self can be enhanced and defined by people's fashion possessions. In virtual worlds, the skins and the garments worn by avatars allow players to express their identities through character choice (Kim et al., 2012). This provides a new landscape for digital fashion, with a focus on the role of the avatar.

2.2 *Virtual Worlds, Avatars and Storytelling: The Role of Player Agency*

Having a virtual avatar is a key component in virtual worlds as it provides a way for users to navigate in the virtual space (Liboriussen, 2011). The avatar allows people to construct and reinvent themselves in virtual worlds (Yee, 2014). Thus, due to the high level of interactivity in these virtual worlds, people can build their own narratives; but these are limited to the rules of the system (Falcão, 2011). Games and virtual worlds convey a sense of presence for players due to their natural state of interactivity (Falcão, 2011). In other words, in games and virtual worlds, players can press buttons, control a character (if any), create worlds, etc.; in sum, the player is an "actor" in this space. This process can be explained through the concept of "player agency". Player agency is a state that emerges as a dynamic response to the interaction with a system (Murray, 2012). This state is usually reflected by a match between the players' actions and the reaction from the "computer"; a mismatch would create frustration, whereas a perfect match would result in a pleasurable experience. This means that self-narratives can be interrelated to the player agency, as in virtual worlds, there are rules that need to be followed (including the world's own narrative). Two processes can be analysed in this case; first, the operational agency (related to the rules of the game) and second, the diegetic agency (related to the narrative of the game) (Falcão, 2011). The diegetic agency is related to player progression (which can take form of quests and levels), role-playing and interactions with the virtual community (which could be other avatars or non-player characters [NPCs]). However, there are many ways in which narratives can be used in games; these might depend on the structure of the game, which can be linear or not. The former supports a levelling up structure whereas the latter allows player decision-making and freedom in the game world (Ip, 2011). This suggests that the diegetic agency could be linear or branched out. These are not the only elements that affect the direction of the narrative. Player emotions also influence the construction of these narratives and could be built through stages or episodes (Ip, 2011). The Hero's Journey is a popular example of the development of game narratives through archetypes such as the hero, mentor, allies and others across three main typical phases: the beginning, the middle and the end (Ip, 2011).

2.3 Brand Storytelling and Story Types: Building Emotional Links with Consumers

According to Smith and Wintrob (2013), brands can use four story "types" to evoke consumer-brand relationships: (1) heritage: related to historical aspects; (2) contemporary: related to innovations; (3) folklore: stories other people tell about the brand and; (4) vision: related to the future perspectives of a brand. Brand stories can be also attached to the narrative of the "loser" or the "winner", in which the brand's founder's story is told via a humble or victorious point of view (Paharia et al., 2011). "Golden legends" (or mythological) archetypes such as the narrative of the "hero", "explorer", "lover" and the "caregiver" can also impact the brand perceived value positively since it evokes emotional connections related to symbolic meaning (Ganassali & Matysiewicz, 2021). This approach has similarities with "The Hero's Journey" and shows that there might be synergies that could be explored when brands enter virtual worlds and develop their own narratives.

Brand stories can be also driven by the brand's reactions towards external factors (Smith & Wintrob, 2013). Thus, this may bring challenges for brands to keep "one" single story alive. The story type and narrative can also influence consumer preferences, depending on the consumer's pre-existing attitudes. For instance, consumers who have malicious envy towards a brand can be affected by the "loser" story style (Kao, 2019). This means that "one" narrative might grab the attention of particular consumers. Ganassali and Matysiewicz (2021) also mentioned that personal stories and consumer involvement might impact brand storytelling; thus, brand storytelling is a two-way communication strategy, which could be enhanced by consumer participation. This moves the perspective of consumer behaviour away for loyalty and satisfaction and more towards emotional consumer behaviour (Akgün et al., 2013), in which virtual worlds and social media play an important role.

2.4 Storytelling Across Different Types of Media

Media convergence is the main paradigm discussed whilst dealing with storytelling across different types of media (Jenkins, 2006). Consumers might extend the narrative towards self-storytelling and content generation across different types of media (Ganassali & Matysiewicz, 2021).

Channel characteristics are a few of the many dimensions that differ media (traditional or new media). In computer-mediated media, telepresence (i.e., the feeling of being part of the environment) is a key differentiator (Novak & Hoffman, 1996). Telepresence is about a mediated experience that is influenced by technological factors such as vividness (e.g., sensory breadth and depth) and interactivity (e.g., speed/response time, range or aspects that can be manipulated and mapping/functionality) (Steuer, 1992). Thus, virtual worlds might offer a lot in terms of telepresence, not just due to the technology, but also due to the interactions they provide (e.g., customisation, avatar creation, world-building, etc.).

Storytelling across different types of media should consider the story as a "whole", built from the parts in each type of media. This premise is built around media convergence (Jenkins, 2006). Story elements that should compose a transmedia narrative are usually driven by characters, conflict (if there are any points of view or relationships), plot (what happens because of the particular conflict), mood (atmosphere) and themes, which would require the development of strategies that address world-building, characterisation, backstory and exposition, audience participation (Zeiser, 2015). This has a strong relationship with games as the narrative might contain ups and downs, similar to the concept of The Hero Journey and the Three-Act structure (beginning, middle and end) (Ip, 2011). Hence, gamification could be connecting mechanism to make the story across different types of media more compelling.

2.5 Storytelling and Gamification

The state of "playfulness" is anchored into unstructured play, whereas the idea of "gamefulness" is based on a rules-structured system (Deterding, 2015). By definition, gamification is the use of game-design elements in non-leisure contexts, such as education, health and marketing (Deterding et al., 2011). Although not all games tell stories (Jenkins, 2004), if a story/narrative is an element of a game, it can be utilised as a gamification strategy. A gamified narrative needs to be built along the user interaction; that is, the player has control over the content experience and does that according to the constraints of the system (e.g., rules and logic) (Toledo Palomino et al., 2019). This shows that player agency has a crucial role in the construction of this narrative when it comes to storytelling in virtual worlds. In this particular case, the narrative construction should be also attached to game-design elements that elicit player progression (Kleinman et al., 2019).

2.6 Online Brand Communities, User-Generated Content and Virtual Worlds

Through transmedia storytelling, consumers evoke real participation and co-creation and spread the word about the brand (Granitz & Forman, 2015). This generates a brand community, or as Muniz and O'Guinn (2001, p. 412) define as a group of "admirers of a brand". Brand communities involve two types of relationships: brand-consumer and consumer-consumer, though the latter tends to be stronger (Muniz & O'Guinn, 2001).

Virtual worlds are a great platform for online communities to emerge. The sense of community and social identity can positively influence brand advocacy and brand love of consumers from luxury brand online communities such as LV and Burberry (Burnasheva et al., 2019). However, research still lacks regarding the different types of platforms that might support particular online communities' activities, social interactions and UGC. Virtual worlds such as SL offer an environment that enhances creativity as it is not bound to one single storyline or quests (Jensen, 2011); SL has its own residents and businesses and it is defined by UGC on its heart.

Therefore, in Fig. 1, we summarise the key concepts that emerged from our initial literature review. Storytelling is mediated by "actors" (brand, brand community and consumer(s)) and the UGC media type (e.g., social media and virtual worlds). Across these elements, there would be space for consumers to co-create with the brand and generate self-stories; at the same time, the brand can utilise the platforms to provide its own narrative. The conceptual framework is exploratory but it aims at providing a foundation to address our research questions.

3 Case Study: *The Ralph Lauren Winter Escape* Experience in *Roblox*

Data has been gathered from media search, the official website of *Ralph Lauren* (RL) corporation, the RL e-commerce website, and the official channels of RL in *Roblox*, and *Twitter. Facebook* and *Pinterest* were not included in this study since the updates in these both channels were

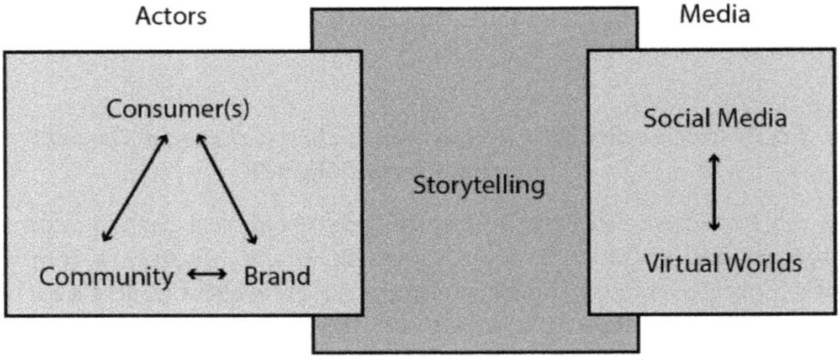

Fig. 1 An exploratory conceptual framework to address brand storytelling in UGC platforms (*Source* Developed by the authors)

out-of-date. *LinkedIn*, *Snapchat*, *YouTube* and *Instagram* were also not included as there were not enough posts relevant for this study.

For this case study, we analyse brand storytelling, brand communication strategies and communities across all the different channels mentioned in the period from 8th December 2021, until 3rd January 2022; the same period that the experience *The Ralph Lauren Winter Escape* (RLWE) took place in *Roblox*.[1]

We utilise the framework emerged from the literature review (see Fig. 1) to undertake the analysis, looking at the role of the actors (consumer(s), brand and community) and characteristics of the media (social media and the virtual worlds) and how storytelling takes form in this environment.

For this particular analysis, we took the experience as the main driver of the story. After that, we have looked at messages in other social media channels to see its repercussion and overarching reactions and integrated stories (if any) through a transmedia storytelling point of view. In order to keep it consistent and relevant for this study, we have selected only the messages that were related to the experience.

[1] Link for the RLWE experience: https://www.roblox.com/games/7608438089/The-Winter-Escape.

3.1 Brand Background

RL is a global brand that has gained a lot of reputation since 1967. Historically, the brand has achieved great exposure and loyalty, particularly through its iconic Polo shirt and the Polo Pony icon. The brand has stated its own five-year strategy in 2018, highlighting keywords such as "authenticity", "timeless style" and sustainable value creation. These core values reflect their own strategic priorities, which include attracting new generations and expand its digital touchpoints.

3.2 Ralph Lauren Winter Escape *(RLWE) Experience*

In 30th September 2021, RL started building its own experience in *Roblox*, called "The Winter Escape" (Ralph Lauren Corporation, 2021). The experience had a total of 4.7M visitors during this period. Half of them rated the experience as positive.

3.3 Media Features

Before entering the experience, players need to interact with the RLWE *Roblox* page. In this page, players can see in a list what they can do, from skating around with other players or to customising hot chocolates in a sponsored RL's virtual truck. The experience also features a limited event in which players can shop for accessories. The page also features possible badges players could collect by collecting rare items. There is also a weekly challenge in which players need to participate in a "Treasure Hunt" and every Monday, they would be able to try new limited items. Outfits can be also purchased using *Robux*.

As soon as the player enters the space, there is a deck with a bench to sit down near a fire. Initially, the player should complete a cheer bar, which would make them stay sometime in the virtual world and collect their first item. By exploring the game world, the player would be able to see the brand at different places, such as a café, a store, etc. The player can also customise their avatar with RL's outfits at any time.

Players can interact with each other using a chat function. Players can also add each other if they want. *Roblox* allows players to see each other's names.

During the experience, the player is invited to join the ice-skating area to play a competitive mini-game. This is a competitive game that restarts after a few minutes and contains a leader board, where players can see each other's names.

The brand utilised *Twitter* to make consumers informed about the weekly rewards at *Roblox*. The hashtags utilised were #RLxRoblox #RLHoliday. *LinkedIn* was used once. The last Tweet about the RLWE was on the 20th December. All the Tweets showed the special items that could be collected in the RLWE. The items advertised in *Twitter* had a nostalgic feeling.

3.4 Story Types and Overall Narrative

The main story in the experience was about enjoying the festive season through RL's sponsorship; players could do this by dressing-up with the brand or just interacting with objects in the world. However, this narrative, supported by brand interactions, was linear and brand-centric. Although players could explore the world and walk to places, or just sit on a chair, they were encouraged to follow quests in order to get rewards, instead of building their own narrative.

There were two crucial points in the experience that resembled a "climax": one, when the player collected the ornaments and was able to decorate the environment and; two, when the player went into the *Treasure Hunt* quest and acquired a new exclusive item.

Audience participation was limited to the chat function and the only items players could customise were their clothes. Therefore, there is not much of UGC in this experience and, with that, little support towards consumer-driven stories. This means that the overall story was centred around the brand. The types of brand stories were had an exploratory tone and were contemporary, historical and vision "stories", which were mostly attached to the items and objects in the world (e.g., *Snow Beach* collection that was launched in the 90s).

The world-building strategy and diegetic agency were aligned with the brand. Although players could choose to play the mini-game or fill the cheer bar, there was not much freedom in the experience. Even if players wanted to wonder around the game, this would fill in the cheer bar and would become another quest completed. The RLWE relied heavily in gamification strategies in order to keep players engaged and coming back to it every day.

3.5 Actors

Roblox is mostly used by young generations. By developing the RLWE, RL could attract young consumers. This fits the overall brand strategy from RL. Authenticity and "timeless" style were also embedded in the experience, particularly in Twitter, where the items were advertised and consumers could read a snippet of the item history. The only narrative that was not included was sustainable value creation.

3.6 Customisation, Engagement and Reward Mechanisms

Players could customise their own avatars and had the choice to pay for outfits or not. It was not imperative to pay for it via in-game "points" or *Robux*. This gave players a sense of agency and self-identity, reflected by the fashion item they worn. Players were encouraged to collect unique items in specific days; so, they would be rewarded by visiting the page on that day. In fact, the whole experience reinforced an action with a particular reward. For instance, by collecting 3 decorations, players could unlock a ticket to the *Treasure Hunt* that would eventually unlock more unique items. In terms of rewards, players could collect items and unlock new items; this was the main system behind the experience. There was no reward by interacting with other players or by creating items in the world.

4 Implications

4.1 Emergent Narratives and the Impact on Consumer-Brand Relationships

Self-stories can be extremely valuable for brands to evoke interaction and emotion relationships (Pera & Viglia, 2016). In our study, there was a lack of engagement with the player's narratives, meaning that there were little consumer-consumer interactions and that the experience felt very individualistic and passive. Although the experience had mixed reviews, with half of the user base rating it as positive, it is possible that RL has not explored the potential of the platform and could consider more the participatory nature of it. However, this may put into question if brands should be exploiting the emergent emotional links that consumers have with each other to build brand trust and relatability. On the other hand, the RL has utilised the festive thematic to draw the narrative and provide a climax for the experience (e.g., when the player impacts the world by decorating it) that resembled some player "participation". Since the experience occurred during the Winter holidays, this showed an alignment of the real-world context and the virtual experience, which could potentially drive consumer co-creation and participation, but players were invited to take a backseat, since they were invited to "play", but nothing more. In sum, there was no UGC.

4.2 The Relationship Between Virtual Worlds and Consumer Co-creation: A Place for Interaction or Exploitation?

The opportunity to customise the avatar in the RLWE was the main interaction that has given the player a sense of agency and autonomy. There were not many options for the player to create or impact the world. Thus, it is not very clear if the experience was an advertising strategy more than a genuine attempt to engage with consumer co-creation.

The utilisation of UGC implies that the consumer's stories need to be incorporated within the brand story in order to build a relationship; otherwise the story is being told by one side (the brand). The RLWE was brand-centric as not much of a narrative emerged from the community. It is possible that individual stories arose, but in this study, it was not possible to capture that. Future research in the area could investigate the role of individual stories and how they merge and blend with the brand story; if there is any alignment or change of perceptions. The RLWE in particular was not built by any Roblox "maker" or "artist", member of the community. As a contrast, *Gucci*, for example, invited a Roblox "artist" to build its experience. Although this chapter has not addressed this, it is possible that RL could have utilised the potential of the platform with a bit more of depth. Since it is a UGC, RLWE had little content generated by its participants. Therefore, it is possible to say that RL had little co-creation activities with consumers. Also, consumer-consumer interactions have not been reinforced by this experience, which may explain the mixed review it has received.

4.3 Measuring the Effect of Consumer-Brand Relationships: When Do Consumers Create Stories and How Do They Share Them?

An opportunity that emerged from our study is the further research into the mapping of virtual communities such as *Roblox* and the motivations of players to interact with the brand. The *Roblox* platform is known to attract young consumers, so by looking at the RLWE, it is suggested RL wanted to engage with this new generation more than selling virtual garments. Netnographic approaches looking at cognitive, emotional and behavioural dimensions could be appropriate to investigate the effectiveness of these experiences. In our study, we have not investigated the impact of the experience on people's perceptions, but this could be addressed in future research. Personality traits and the sense of ownership in virtual luxury fashion could be also discussed.

4.4 The Emergent Relationship Between Gamification and Luxury Fashion Goods

Luxury implies collecting and owning unique items. An approach for further research could be understanding the relationship between owning items and luxury consumer behaviour from an ethnographic lens, looking at social elements, cultural aspects, brand communities and storytelling. Since there is a rise on digital fashion, this blurs the line between item collection in games (which can be related to the game strategy) and a sense of status and digital identity. Emergent narratives based on players' motivations could be explored further, since players might be motivated by collecting rare fashion items and by being fashionable or feeling they belong to a brand community.

5 Conclusion

This chapter aimed at addressing three exploratory research questions, from which findings can be summarised below:

- Our case study has shown that luxury fashion brands (e.g., RL in our case) tend to use virtual communities to tell stories in a format of event that happens during a specific time (similar to an exhibition); whereas social media channels such as Twitter, are used to communicate consumers about these events and motivate them to visit the virtual worlds/events.
- Roblox is a platform built on UGC, however there was little content generated by the community itself in the case studied in this chapter. However, fashion brands have been using the Roblox platform to get closer to its target market.

- The factors that affect brand storytelling across different channels are related to the affordances of each channel. That is, Roblox, for instance, allows consumers to play with the brands, customise their characters/avatars, explore new looks and interact with other consumers in a virtual world. Other channels like Twitter do not have such features. Fashion brands could work together with consumers in virtual platforms to generate stories together.

The RLWE case illustrates the social media marketing activities mentioned by Kim and Ko (2012) since it provides an opportunity for consumers to have fun with the brand, interactivity, trendiness (e.g., festive season) and customisation; though there was not much evidence of word of mouth in this particular experience. It is not very clear if the RLWE was effective. On the other hand, the RLWE has been featured in the RL official corporate page as an innovative strategy, which supports the brand story and mission. Was the experience compelling and engaging for the players? Or did RL created this experience to utilise a huge potential consumer base to build brand awareness? These questions arise as brands are rushing to conquer the "metaverse" and be the first to get there. Also, the potential consumer base in platforms such as *Roblox* and *Fortnite* is accessible for brands and creating experiences in these online spaces is not costly, if compared to other types of advertising.

Fashion consumer behaviour in the real world can be mimicked in the digital world as the avatar becomes a valuable item of self-representation (Yee, 2014). Consumers can buy digital outfits in places such as *Roblox*, and spend thousands of dollars in one item. This brings ethical debates as there is a trend for expenditure in digital fashion, mostly represented by the rise of Non-Fungible Tokens (NFTs) (i.e., digital tokens that can be represented by digital art stored in a blockchain that can be sold and traded), supported by an unsustainable system, which can make a lot of people lose money. Thus, consumers need to be critical and understand the implications of their interactions in virtual worlds. Choices and interactions need to be transparent. Yet, many challenges still remain. The brand story cannot be only sustained by one side of the narrative; consumers' experiences and self-narratives also impact brand storytelling.

References

Akgün, A. E., Koçoğlu, İ., & İmamoğlu, S. Z. (2013). An emerging consumer experience: Emotional branding. *Procedia—Social and Behavioral Sciences, 99*, 503–508. https://doi.org/10.1016/j.sbspro.2013.10.519

Burnasheva, R., Suh, Y. G., & Villalobos-Moron, K. (2019). Sense of community and social identity effect on brand love: Based on the online communities of a luxury fashion brands. *Journal of Global Fashion Marketing, 10*(1), 50–65. https://doi.org/10.1080/20932685.2018.1558087

Chu, S. C., & Seock, Y. K. (2020). The power of social media in fashion advertising. *Journal of Interactive Advertising, 20*(2), 93–94. https://doi.org/10.1080/15252019.2020.1802955

Deterding, S. (2015). The lens of intrinsic skill atoms: A method for gameful design. *Human-Computer Interaction, 30*(3–4), 294–335. https://doi.org/10.1080/07370024.2014.993471

Deterding, S., Dixon, D., Khaled, R., & Nacke, L. (2011). *From game design elements to gamefulness*. Proceedings of the 15th International Academic MindTrek Conference on Envisioning Future Media Environments—MindTrek '11, 9. https://doi.org/10.1145/2181037.2181040

Dredge, S. (2019, September 28). All you need to know about Roblox | Games. *The Guardian*. https://www.theguardian.com/games/2019/sep/28/roblox-guide-children-gaming-platform-developer-minecraft-fortnite

Falcão, T. (2011). Structures of agency in virtual worlds. In N. Zagalo, L. Morgado, & A. Boa-Ventura (Eds.), *Virtual worlds and metaverse platforms: New communication and identity paradigms* (pp. 192–205). IGI Global. https://doi.org/10.4018/978-1-60960-854-5.ch013

Felix, R., Rauschnabel, P. A., & Hinsch, C. (2017). Elements of strategic social media marketing: A holistic framework. *Journal of Business Research, 70*, 118–126. https://doi.org/10.1016/J.JBUSRES.2016.05.001

Ganassali, S., & Matysiewicz, J. (2021). Echoing the golden legends: Storytelling archetypes and their impact on brand perceived value. *Journal of Marketing Management, 37*(5–6), 437–463. https://doi.org/10.1080/0267257X.2020.1831577

Granitz, N., & Forman, H. (2015). Building self-brand connections: Exploring brand stories through a transmedia perspective. *Journal of Brand Management, 22*(1), 38–59. https://doi.org/10.1057/BM.2015.1/TABLES/2

Hackl, C. (2020). *Social VR, Facebook Horizon and the future of social media marketing*. https://www.forbes.com/sites/cathyhackl/2020/08/30/social-vr-facebook-horizon--the-future-of-social-media-marketing/?sh=425375e65b19

Ip, B. (2011). Narrative structures in computer and video games: Part 1: Context, definitions, and initial findings. *Games and Culture, 6*(2), 103–134. https://doi.org/10.1177/1555412010364982

Jenkins, H. (2004). Game design as narrative architecture. *Computer, 44*, 1–15.
Jenkins, H. (2006). *Convergence culture: Where old and new media collide*. New York University Press.
Jensen, S. S. (2011). User-driven content creation in second life a source of innovation? In N. Zagalo, L. Morgado, & A. Boa-Ventura (Eds.), *Virtual worlds and metaverse platforms: New communication and identity paradigms*. IGI Global. https://doi.org/10.4018/978-1-60960-854-5.ch001
Kao, D. T. (2019). The impact of envy on brand preference: Brand storytelling and psychological distance as moderators. *Journal of Product and Brand Management, 28*(4), 515–528. https://doi.org/10.1108/JPBM-08-2018-2004/FULL/PDF
Kim, A. J., & Ko, E. (2012). Do social media marketing activities enhance customer equity? An empirical study of luxury fashion brand. *Journal of Business Research, 65*(10), 1480–1486. https://doi.org/10.1016/j.jbusres.2011.10.014
Kim, S. J., Kim, K. H., & Mattila, P. (2012). The role of fashion in the characters of online games. *Journal of Global Fashion Marketing, 3*(2), 81–88. https://doi.org/10.1080/20932685.2012.10593110
Kleinman, E., Carstensdottir, E., & Seif El-Nasr, M. (2019). *A model for analyzing diegesis in digital narrative games*. Lecture Notes in Computer Science (Including Subseries Lecture Notes in Artificial Intelligence and Lecture Notes in Bioinformatics), 11869 LNCS, pp. 8–21. https://doi.org/10.1007/978-3-030-33894-7_2
Koster, R. (2021). *Online world or metaverse?* Raph's Website. https://www.raphkoster.com/2021/09/02/online-world-or-metaverse/
Liboriussen, B. (2011). Collective building projects in second life: User motives and strategies explained from an architectural and ethnographic perspective. In N. Zagalo, L. Morgado, & A. Boa-Ventura (Eds.), *Virtual worlds and metaverse platforms: New communication and identity paradigms* (pp. 33–46). IGI Global. https://doi.org/10.4018/978-1-60960-854-5.ch003
Loussaïef, L., Ulrich, I., & Damay, C. (2019). How does access to luxury fashion challenge self-identity? Exploring women's practices of joint and non-ownership. *Journal of Business Research, 102*, 263–272. https://doi.org/10.1016/J.JBUSRES.2019.02.020
Muniz, A. M., & O'Guinn, T. C. (2001). Brand community. *Journal of Consumer Research, 27*(4), 412–432.
Murray, J. H. (2012). *Inventing the medium: Principles of interaction design as a cultural practice*. The MIT Press. http://www.jstor.org/stable/j.ctt5hhjgg
Novak, T. P., & Hoffman, D. L. (1996). Marketing in hypermedia computer-mediated environments: Conceptual foundations. *Journal of Marketing, 60*(3), 50–68.

Paharia, N., Keinan, A., Avery, J., & Schor, J. B. (2011). The underdog effect: The marketing of disadvantage and determination through brand biography. *Journal of Consumer Research, 37*(5), 775–790. https://doi.org/10.1086/656219

Pera, R., & Viglia, G. (2016). Exploring how video digital storytelling builds relationship experiences. *Psychology & Marketing, 33*(12), 1142–1150. https://doi.org/10.1002/MAR.20951

Ralph Lauren Corporation. (2021). *Ralph Lauren creates expansive holiday-themed experience on Roblox*. https://corporate.ralphlauren.com/pr_211208_Roblox.html

Roach, J. (2021). *What is Fortnite?* Digital Trends. https://www.digitaltrends.com/gaming/what-is-fortnite/

Robertson, A., & Peters, J. (2021). *What is the metaverse, and do I have to care?* The Verge. https://www.theverge.com/22701104/metaverse-explained-fortnite-roblox-facebook-horizon

Roblox. (2021). *The Gucci Garden experience lands on Roblox*. Roblox Blog. https://blog.roblox.com/2021/05/gucci-garden-experience/

Smith, A. N., Fischer, E., & Yongjian, C. (2012). How does brand-related user-generated content differ across YouTube, Facebook, and Twitter? *Journal of Interactive Marketing, 26*(2), 102–113. https://doi.org/10.1016/J.INTMAR.2012.01.002

Smith, K., & Wintrob, M. (2013). Brand storytelling: A framework for activation. *Design Management Review, 24*(1), 36–41. https://doi.org/10.1111/drev.10227

Steuer, J. (1992). Defining virtual reality: Dimensions determining telepresence. *Journal of Communication, 42*(4), 73–93. https://doi.org/10.1111/j.1460-2466.1992.tb00812.x

The Fortnite Team. (2020). *What is Fortnite? Beginner's guide*. https://www.epicgames.com/fortnite/en-US/news/what-is-fortnite-beginners-guide

Toledo Palomino, P., Toda, A. M., Oliveira, W., Cristea, A. I., & Isotani, S. (2019). *Narrative for gamification in education: Why should you care?* Proceedings—IEEE 19th International Conference on Advanced Learning Technologies, ICALT 2019. https://doi.org/10.1109/ICALT.2019.00035

Venkatesh, A., Joy, A., Sherry, J. F., Jr., & Deschenes, J. (2010). The aesthetics of luxury fashion, body and identify formation. *Journal of Consumer Psychology, 20*(4), 459–470. https://doi.org/10.1016/j.jcps.2010.06.011

Webster, A. (2021). *Ariana Grande's Fortnite tour was a moment years in the making*. The Verge. https://www.theverge.com/2021/8/9/22616664/ariana-grande-fortnite-rift-tour-worldbuilding-storytelling

Woo, A., & Forbes Agency Council. (2021). *Mapping the metaverse: How can brands make the most of this new world?* https://www.forbes.com/sites/forbesagencycouncil/2021/11/30/mapping-the-metaverse-how-can-brands-make-the-most-of-this-new-world/?sh=3edd3fdb6534

Woodside, A. G. (2010). Brand-consumer storytelling theory and research: Introduction to a Psychology & Marketing special issue. *Psychology and Marketing, 27*(6), 531–540. https://doi.org/10.1002/mar.20342

Yee, N. (2014). *The Proteus paradox: How online games and virtual worlds change us—And how they don't*. Yale Univeristy Press.

Zeiser, A. (2015). Transmedia marketing: From film and TV to games and digital media. In *Transmedia marketing*. https://www.proquest.com/books/transmedia-marketing/docview/2148110801/se-2?accountid=11526%0Ahttps://hud.alma.exlibrisgroup.com/discovery/openurl?institution=44HUD_INST&vid=44HUD_INST:Services&sid=ProQ%3Aebookcentral1&genre=book&issn=&volume=&issue=&spag

CHAPTER 4

The Use of Augmented Reality to Enhance Consumer Experience: The Case of Kohl's Snapchat Virtual Closet and Sephora Virtual Artist

Vanissa Wanick, James Stallwood, and Eirini Bazaki

Abstract The pandemic has forced fashion brands to find alternatives to provide more engaging online consumer experiences, particularly through emerging technologies such as Augmented Reality (AR). The Virtual Fitting Room (VFR) is an example of that. Consumers can try fashion products and interact with them without having to visit a store. This chapter addresses the use of AR try-on services by fashion brands with

V. Wanick (✉) · J. Stallwood · E. Bazaki
Winchester School of Art, University of Southampton, Southampton, UK
e-mail: vwv1n12@soton.ac.uk; v.w.vieira@soton.ac.uk

J. Stallwood
e-mail: J.E.Stallwood@soton.ac.uk

E. Bazaki
e-mail: E.Bazaki@soton.ac.uk

E. Bazaki and V. Wanick (eds.), *Reinventing Fashion Retailing*, Palgrave Studies in Practice: Global Fashion Brand Management ,
https://doi.org/10.1007/978-3-031-11185-3_4

the aim to enhance the consumer experience. This chapter aims at providing a set of recommendations for fashion brands to employ AR within their brand strategy through a multi-case study approach. Two cases were analysed: *Kohl's Snapchat Virtual Closet* (KSVC), released in 2020, and *Sephora Virtual Artist* (SVA), released in 2017. First, we start by analysing the consumer journey in each of the cases, including the characteristics of the brand and the technological features; this is followed by a comparison between the cases. Five themes emerged from our analysis: social media integration and brand congruency, consumer agency and flow experience, narrative experiences and omnichannel orchestration and inclusive design and sustainable fashion. Implications for both practice and theory are discussed. We finish the chapter with recommendations and insights about the use of AR for fashion brands, including emergent themes such as adaptive fashion.

Keywords Augmented reality · Consumer experience · Virtual fitting room · Adaptive fashion · Consumer agency

1 Introduction

The global Virtual Fitting Room (VFR) market size is projected to reach USD 10.00 billion by 2027, exhibiting a CAGR of 20.1% during the forecast period (Fortune Business Insights, 2020). Boosted by the 2020's global pandemic, the VFR can be a great opportunity for retailers to provide a holistic consumer experience. The VFR can provide a few advantages for consumers and retailers, such as convenience, online sales support, consumer connection and return rate reduction (Dopson, 2021). The VFR is very similar to the physical in-store changing room, which provides an active way for buyers to try attires, accessories and other things virtually instead of tangible. By using Augmented Reality (AR) technology through overlaying an apparel or an accessory onto the mirror copy of the shopper, VFRs are becoming each time more popular. For instance, in 2020, *Gucci* has partnered with *Snapchat* for an AR shoe try-on experience that reached 18.9 million people across the globe. By using *Snapchat's* lens features, users could play with different digital "shoes" and purchase them directly from the app (Snap Inc., 2020).

AR technology is revolutionising the fashion industry as it is enhancing customer shopping experience, without requiring shoppers to move from the comfort of their homes. The entry of AR and the expansion of e-commerce platforms have brought virtual fitting rooms to the fore and clothing giants around the world are heartily embracing this technological turnaround. In 2017, *Gap* launched an AR app called *DressingRoom*, which allows customers to try on clothes remotely (Fortune Business Insights, 2020). Also, in 2017, *Sephora* introduced the *Sephora Virtual Artist* (SVA) AR feature that scans users' face and allows them to try different types of makeup (Carman, 2017). In 2019, *Amazon* announced the development of a VFR platform to allow customers to try out clothes of their choice before buying them through an Artificial Intelligence (AI) systems (e.g., computer vision and Generative Adversarial Networks (GAN)) (Wiggers, 2020). Also in 2019, *Google* announced an AR try-on makeup service for consumers to try advertised products whilst watching videos from influencers in *YouTube* (Luber, 2019). In 2020, *Google* expanded the service for general searches, working with other service providers such as *ModiFace* (the same service provider of *Sephora's Virtual Artist*), transforming each product search into a more immersive experience (Kannan, 2020).

AR-powered virtual fitting rooms are enabling retail brands to engage potential customers and widen their sales horizons. At the same time, complying with social distancing rules set by the coronavirus global pandemic, fashion brands have been forced to seal off their trial rooms. In March 2020, Kohl's, the American retail chain announced the closure of its trial rooms (Fortune Business Insights, 2020). Although the world is aiming at going back to normality after the pandemic, this presents a unique opportunity for companies to promote their VFR platforms as they can ensure that customers are able to enjoy the full trial-room experience virtually and make an informed purchase decision. Therefore, this chapter aims at addressing the following exploratory questions:

- What is the value of this experience for consumers?
- What can fashion brands explore in this digital environment?
- How effective these strategies might be? Who can benefit from it?

This chapter presents *Kohl's Snapchat Virtual Closet* and *Sephora Virtual Artist* case studies, through an in-depth analysis, contrasting and comparing fashion management strategies utilised by each brand. The chapter finalises with an in-depth discussion addressing current challenges regarding this type of technology in fashion and proposes a case to support the use of AR for inclusive consumer experiences.

2 Background

AR combines both real and virtual elements in real time through 3D interactive dimensions (Azuma, 1997). In 1997, Azuma (1997) published a seminal work around the use of AR in different environments such medical and manufacturing purposes. At that time, AR was considered a new field and its use through mobile phone cameras was not mentioned as a potential use case. Almost 30 years later, challenges still remain. For instance, experiences through AR technologies are still very limited to one sense (sight). Azuma (1997) mentioned that AR should not be limited to sight, and other senses could be enhanced by the use of this type of technology. This is crucial in order to convey inclusive experiences. If AR is limited to sight, then users with visual impairments will be left out of the experience.

The AR realm is, however, in constant transformation and moving towards a more human-centric approach. This overlay of digital assets to the physical world can be coined as the first wave of AR, whereas the second wave is centred around more human, immersive and sensorial experiences (Papagiannis, 2018). This shows a shift of paradigm. For instance, Papagiannis (2018) demonstrates in her book that AR can actually help people with visual impairments to "see" through vibration sensors in a smartphone. This could be insightful for fashion brands to include tactile experiences in AR so that consumers can "touch" the garments' fabric "virtually". Although not much has been mentioned about the costs of developing such technologies and making them available to the mass market, these examples show great potential of AR to enhance brand experiences.

AR offers a new layer of interaction for consumer behaviour. There are different ways by which consumers can interact with AR technologies in retail. For example, consumers can interact with AR by adding virtual products in their environment through try-on applications or they can scan logos or visuals to look for additional content about a brand or product (Javornik, 2016). These interactive layers take form by three physical elements: an individual or person (e.g., by overlaying virtual garments or makeup), products (e.g., by scanning a product and unlocking virtual content) or the environment or space (e.g., by placing virtual objects in a room) (Javornik, 2016). According to Javornik (2016), although AR can be a promising technological feature to increase brand interactivity, there are limitations to its use such as social connectivity. Challenges regarding the role of the salesperson, for example, might still remain, but could be addressed via the integration of the virtual room within VR or in-store magic mirrors (Bazaki & Wanick, 2019) (see Fig. 1). However, differently from social media, AR provides fewer social elements that might be required in order to promote social identity and a high level of relationship with the brand.

AR implementations in retail might differ. For instance, for beauty products and cosmetics, AR can function as a virtual try-on; whereas for clothing brands, AR can be used via try-on mirrors (in physical stores) (Watson et al., 2018). The main take away from the use of AR in retail is that its highly sensorial experience might increase consumers' attitude towards a brand, influencing their purchase intentions positively. In fact, Watson et al. (2018) found that the use of AR might be even more effective for cosmetics and fashion product categories, due to its hedonic motivational nature, which involves concepts like enjoyment and playfulness. This suggests that VFRs can improve consumer experience as they might provide a sense of fun and pleasure. VFRs may also decrease the amount of returns as one of the biggest issues with online retail is a bad fit (Lee & Xu, 2020). Yet, VFRs would need to be extremely accurate in order to provide the correct body measurements. Thus, it is not very clear how fashion brands could use AR for. Although VFRs can enhance both utilitarian and hedonic aspects, this might be related to the type of technology utilised (e.g., if the VFR is more accurate, it may enhance utilitarian experiences). Therefore, this chapter aims at providing an illustrative discussion about the benefits and challenges of the use of AR by fashion retailers and provide a list of recommendations for its use.

Digital platforms allow consumers to experience high levels of brand interactivity (Lee et al., 2013). Brand experiences enhanced by digital touchpoints can be enacted during different stages of the consumer journey, such as pre-purchase, purchase and post-purchase, and might depend on the type of technology utilised (Wanick et al., 2017). AR applications, such as the geolocated mobile game *Pokémon Go* can help brands to engage with consumers in the pre-purchase stage (Wanick et al., 2017). For example, in 2016, *Starbucks* announced a partnership with *Pokémon*

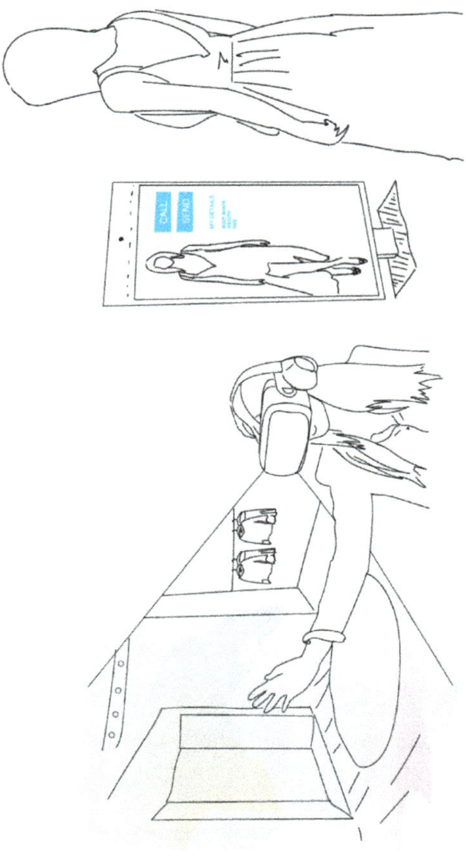

Fig. 1 VR fitting room experience (left) and Magic Mirror (right) (*Source* Bazaki & Wanick, 2019)

Go, in which consumers could locate a store via the app and discover and order a special *Frappuccino* flavoured drink as a reward (Starbucks, 2016). This strategy showed an integration of the pre-purchase with the actual purchase stage, as consumers were "guided" by the app to purchase the drink. Gamification (i.e., the use of game elements in non-leisure contexts [Deterding et al., 2011]) was also used in combination with AR, in order to provide rewards and increase consumer engagement.

3 Case Study Structure and Case Selection

To understand the use of AR in fashion and address the research questions mentioned in the introduction of this chapter, we have selected two case studies. In line with Watson et al.'s (2018) work, we have selected a fashion case and a beauty/cosmetics case, since these are two brand categories that have been utilising AR technologies for consumer engagement. The cases are structured by an overview of the brand, its placement and a description of the brand strategy using AR platforms. The data utilised to construct the cases were gathered from Kohl's and Sephora's official websites as well as news articles published about both brand strategies.

3.1 Case Study 1: Kohl's Snapchat Virtual Closet

Kohl's is an American department store founded in 1962 that went public in 1992. In 20 years, Kohl's has managed to grow and so far, they own more than 1,100 stores across the U.S. The e-commerce platform, Kohls.com, promotes an omnichannel consumer experience, in which consumers can conveniently shop online. The company offers a variety of brands in their portfolio. Kohl's targets the family market of active wellness, including the beauty business, with offers of skin care, fragrance, makeup and personal care (Kohl's, 2020a).

In May 2020, Kohl's has collaborated with *Snapchat* (Kohl's, 2020b) to create *Kohl's AR Virtual Closet*. As a strategy to attract young consumers, Kohl's found in *Snapchat* a great platform. According to Statista, the USA is the largest country with Snapchat users, with 108mi users (Statista Research Department, 2022). The *Snapchat* audience is 381.5mi globally. Age group is 25–34, with more than 88 million users in this age range (Hootsuite, 2020). By using a smartphone and the *Snapchat* app, consumers were able to step inside an AR dressing room, mixing and matching items, and making a purchase without leaving the app or their home.

Items available for purchase in the *Kohl's AR Virtual Closet* were continually updated based on consumer needs. The experience launched with top spring styles and shifted to an assortment of active and athleisure items as shoppers searched for comfortable work-from-home apparel. For instance, one iteration featured back-to-school season items with a collaboration assortment of Levi's products. Customers can also use the "Selfie Lens" feature to picture themselves in the *Levi's Trucker Jacket*. This highlights the integration between the AR feature and the social media platform as lenses are a very characteristic feature in Snapchat.

As much as Kohl's have utilised Snapchat to get closer to their target market, the discoverability of the lens might have been an issue. Without any supporting advertising campaign or media coverage, it could be difficult for consumers to find the Virtual Closet by only navigating the platform or depending on social media shares from friends or brand communities. Different from other VFRs in the market, Kohl's strategy had an advertising dependency since it was not an embedded feature within an app or a standalone app. Thus, this strategy shows more aspects related to playful experiences rather than utilitarian shopping.

3.2 Case Study 2: Sephora's Virtual Artist

Sephora is a French beauty brand that belongs to the luxury group Louis Vuitton Moet Hennessy (LVMH). The brand was founded in 1969 by Dominique Maudonnaud. Differently from Kohl's, the *Sephora's Virtual Artist* is a standalone mobile app that can be downloaded directly from app stores.[1] The app allows consumers to choose a product that overlays onto the user's face using the phone camera. The app was launched in 2017, via an update in the current *Sephora's* official app. The demo of the app showed the possibility to share the overlayed options of makeup with friends using the hashtag #sephoravirtualartist. Although the app was launched in 2017, the "Virtual Artist" feature was adopted by physical stores to avoid makeup contamination after the COVID-19 global pandemic, showing a potential use for AR mobile try-ons, even in-store.

[1] At the time of writing this chapter, the app was not available anymore (only in Singapore). We have utilised the walkthrough video with features from the official *ModiFace* and *Sephora's* channel and published articles to underline the overall experience.

Sephora was not the first makeup brand to utilise this type of technology. In 2016, Rimmel's app "Get the Look" introduced the same features; consumers could place the virtual makeup over their faces through the mobile camera and purchase the products after trying them on (Watson et al., 2018). The *Sephora Virtual Artist* was developed by the service provider *ModiFace*, which has developed experiences to other beauty brands, such as L'Oreal and Armani and provides other services integrated with social media apps (e.g., *Instagram* and *WeChat*).

4 Discussion

4.1 Social Media Integration and Brand Congruency

Kohl's case shows a successful integration between the platform and the brand strategy. Since Snapchat is largely used by young consumers, Kohl's developed a strategy accessible to its audience. Social shopping in this case was managed through the sharing tools and filters enabled by the app. The same could be seen in SVA, as users can share their makeup looks using a hashtag.

Shopping is a social process in which the salesperson can enhance the consumer experience. This is crucial for brand management since shopping with a companion tends to enhance the consumer experience (Merrilees & Miller, 2019). However, when considering the social anthropological perspective of the VFR, there is no feature that invites a second, third person into the fitting room. Consumers can still share screen shots of their fitting with their friends, but this requires additional effort, there might be time differences between when a friend sees the photo and when they respond to it. Thus, this limits the social aspect of the shopping experience. Additionally, many brands rely on collaborations with apps for the use of the virtual fitting room; yet, the adoption of those apps is also limited to a specific target audience, which suggests that Kohl's case was not targeted to a wider audience.

Accuracy, attractiveness and interactivity are elements that affect consumer behaviour whilst interacting with VFRs (Lee & Xu, 2020). When considering consumer experience, it is possible to categorise VFRs into seven categories: full 3D body scanner, 3D avatar, 3D customer model, photo-accurate 3D customer model, robotic mannequin, AR fitting room and VR fitting room (Lee & Xu, 2020). This shows that when discussing the VFR, it is important to consider the type of technology utilised since each one would provide a different experience to the consumer. The AR type of VFR is the most popular one so far and can also enhance hedonic and utilitarian aspects of consumer behaviour (Lee & Xu, 2020).

4.2 *The Humanisation of the Brand Experience*

Another aspect to consider is the humanisation and the personalisation of the VFR experience. One example is the use of human avatars. The development and virtual fittings for consumers to better understand whether a product fits through human avatars could be effective to convey such "humanisation" to the experience (Muta et al., 2018; Polke & Kumari, 2018). The VFR also provides the possibility for consumers to decorate themselves. This produces not just a sense of body ownership, but also autonomy and a high level of engagement and enjoyment during the e-shopping experience (Huang & Liao, 2017).

In Kohl's case, there is no use of avatar since the consumer uses their camera to interact with the app through AR technologies; that is the application places the garments on the top of the user's body through the camera. This might allow consumers to have a more accurate view of the fitting.

In the case of SVA, research has shown that the incorporation of AR elements in consumer's space can provide an intimate and relaxing environment as the experience feels personal (Scholz & Duffy, 2018).

4.3 *Consumer Agency and Flow Experience*

VFR can enhance hedonic experiences of consumers, since the platform can be fun and enjoyable due to its high level of interactivity (Lee & Xu, 2020). Both hedonic and utilitarian shopping values are related to flow (i.e., "optimal experiences" as defined by Csikszentmihalyi [2008]) that consumers have whilst shopping online (Bridges, 2018). This means that consumers who experience hedonic flow tend to lose track of time and "escape" from reality, whereas utilitarian flow dimensions include skills and abilities to be able to make a purchase. However, as online experiences get more mainstream, it might be difficult to separate hedonic from utilitarian dimensions; thus, looking at flow as a particular factor that contributes for consumer experience is crucial (Bridges, 2018). In online environments, flow is conveyed by both personal and social interactions (Choi & Kim, 2004). Therefore, it is suggested that social elements need to be included in VFR experiences. Another aspect to consider when looking at flow experiences is usability. How easy it is to use the VFR portrayed by Kohl's and Sephora's case? What is the use case?

4.4 *Narrative Experience and Omnichannel Orchestration*

Consumers value experiences that address a narrative in AR environments. This narrative can be conveyed by navigation, graphic features and information content, mostly showing the chronological order of interactions (Huang & Liu, 2014). Although Kohl's case shows potential integration with social media, there is not a way of visualising a narrative. This suggests that for VFR strategies to be more effective, they should consider exploring different channels. On the other hand, Sephora's Virtual Artist has been applied in physical stores to provide more health and safety conditions for consumers, avoiding contamination from shared makeup. This shows that the VFR has another utility that goes beyond hedonic and utilitarian factors as it can provide a sense of trust.

4.5 *Augmenting Which Reality?*

AR means *Augmented* Reality and the word *augmented* should be emphasised. AR is about enhancing elements from the physical world environment directly or indirectly (Carmigniani et al., 2011). Thus, if the interactions are not usable or accessible, this physical reality has not been enhanced. However, it is not just the accessibility of the AR app that needs to be considered; it is which reality feature that needs to be augmented. The virtual information brought by AR applications should simplify and help users make decisions (Carmigniani et al., 2011). Therefore, AR is not a replacement or a replication of already existing aspects of the real-world interaction, but its enhancement/augmentation. This is part of the "Entryway" or the second wave of AR, as Papagiannis (2018) points out in her seminal book; this new wave is human-centred.

5 Implications

AR applied to fashion has the potential to influence hedonic motivations due to its sensory richness (Watson et al., 2018). Kohl's case showed great integration with the brand's target audience. However, accessibility is an issue that has not been considered. The VFR is integrated in an app filter and depends on discoverability and the commitment of consumers with the brand community. This participation in the virtual community is attached to the concept of trust. For example, the level of communication in the virtual community helps consumers to build brand trust (Casaló et al., 2008). As much as having a VFR attached to a well-known app such as Snapchat, it is possible that the VFR function could have been blurred with advertising purposes, such as increasing the eWOM power of the brand message. In fact, by providing opportunities for consumers to experiment with the brand could enhance the way they see themselves and therefore contribute for positive eWOM. Due to a consumer-creation approach, consumers can evoke self-construal feelings, which impact eWOM in virtual communities (Lee et al., 2012).

Another aspect to consider is collaboration within omnichannel experiences (Salazar, 2021). Collaboration across channels can enrich consumer experience as it divides channels according to their roles (e.g., target channels and helper channels), reducing costs of interaction.

Consumer agency was another aspect that emerged from the analysis of the cases. By allowing consumers to manipulate objects and make choices, this could enhance their sense of self. Marketers should consider leaving the transactional nature of the brand experience in the background and utilise AR to reinforce consumer's sense of self (Scholz & Duffy, 2018). Thus, it might be that there is a potential for fashion retailers to expand its reach and develop more inclusive try-on opportunities. For instance, consumers with disabilities might find value on AR try-on services as they might be able to try clothes without having to physically change; this might speed up the process and make them have a more positive experience.

5.1 For Theory

AR applications in fashion can go beyond its utilitarian and hedonic values and experiences. Since these applications might convey a sense of self, research in the area could investigate more about self-congruity of these apps, including how to enhance the sense of self for consumer with disabilities, which is an overlooked market. This not just make the fashion industry more inclusive, but it may enhance its corporate social responsibility values.

It is also crucial to understand how the use of the VFRs can be integrated with the whole consumer journey. It is not very clear yet if all consumers end up buying the product after interacting with it online.

Haptics, taste and smell need to be added to the list of features that need to be considered whilst moving these applications to another level. For instance, AR devices such as *Scentee* (a small device that can be coupled with a smartphone) can be utilised to release scents and smells (Papagiannis, 2018), enhancing multi-sensory experiences that generates consumer value (Hultén, 2011).

5.2 For Practice

Consumers with disabilities might find difficult to try on clothes and to feel the sense of self that goes beyond the transactional nature of the brand experience. This is a new area to be explored. Coined as "Adaptive Fashion", the global market for this trend is expected to reach $400bi by 2026 (Jordan, 2021). This is in fact, a reality, as 1.2 billion of people in the world have disabilities and that accounts for 15% of the global population (WeThe15, 2021).

Another aspect that should be enhanced by the VFRs is to be more inclusive towards its body measurements. Plus-size consumers might find difficult to look for garments that fit them well. Thus, investing in accuracy of measurements and algorithms that learn from non-biased data sets should be included in research and development processes.

Another aspect to mention is that both cases selected in this chapter and the cases mentioned in the literature have been designed for brand new products. So far, VFRs have not been applied for second-hand garments businesses, which are usually e-commerce based (e.g., eBay, Depop, Vinted) and could benefit from standard VFR services. Yet, the accuracy of VFRs could contribute for fashion sustainability; if the virtual fit is precise, then there would be less returns. It could be possible that if the digital experience is accurate, garments could be ordered and made by request. This would reinforce ethical fashion, the slow fashion movement (Donaldson, 2020) and the business of fashion artisans. As designers can tweak and make adjustments on digital garments, this could potentially decrease waste (Agence France-Presse, 2022), thus making fashion more sustainable.

6 Conclusion

This chapter aimed at addressing three exploratory research questions, from which findings can be summarised below:

- Our findings show that AR and VFR strategies can influence consumer behaviour on the emotional level; it is very unlikely that consumers would purchase items via these applications. From our study, we also found a potential for fashion brands to utilise AR and VFR to make the consumer experience more inclusive and accessible.
- Fashion brands can explore AR and VFR to build more humane relationships with consumers. Other strategies might also consider the orchestration of touchpoints by building hybrid communications with consumers. Fashion brands can also provide more agency to consumers via these apps, but the current technologies might not be yet accessible by the mass market.
- AR and VFR strategies can be very effective to build emotional links with consumers if the experience is positive. This is due to the playfulness of the current apps, which allow consumers to manipulate the brand and develop a sense of agency and creativity. On the other hand, AR and VFR are yet still not accessible to all.

To conclude, our findings have shown that using Augmented Reality (AR) has great potential for promoting consumer behaviour, but it can also unlock other promising areas, such as adaptive/inclusive fashion and sustainable fashion. In sum, AR, when done right, can have a great impact on people's attitudes: a positive experience encourages the shopper to buy it, whereas a negative experience produces an opposite effect. AR in this space can be used with many factors involved when the shopper makes one choice or another and has been shown to have relative effectiveness in doing just that.

References

Agence France-Presse. (2022). Fashion industry looks to online metaverse as test lab for developing new products, blurring the line between virtual and real. *South China Morning Post*. https://www.scmp.com/lifestyle/fashion-beauty/article/3163424/fashion-industry-looks-online-metaverse-test-lab

Azuma, R. T. (1997). A survey of augmented reality. *Presence, 6*(4), 355–385. https://doi.org/10.1162/pres.1997.6.4.355

Bazaki, E., & Wanick, V. (2019). Unlocking the potential of the salesperson in the virtual fitting room: Enhancing the online retail experience for fashion brands. In *academy for design innovation management conference 2019 London* (p. 11). Academy for Design Innovation Management.

Bridges, E. (2018). Hedonic and utilitarian shopping goals: A decade later. *Journal of Global Scholars of Marketing Science, 28*(3), 282–290. https://doi.org/10.1080/21639159.2018.1439398

Carman, A. (2017). *Sephora's latest app update lets you try virtual makeup on at home with AR*. The Verge. https://www.theverge.com/2017/3/16/14946086/sephora-virtual-assistant-ios-app-update-ar-makeup

Carmigniani, J., Furht, B., Anisetti, M., Ceravolo, P., Damiani, E., & Ivkovic, M. (2011). Augmented reality technologies, systems and applications. *Multimedia Tools and Applications, 51*(1), 341–377. https://doi.org/10.1007/s11042-010-0660-6

Casaló, L. V., Flavián, C., & Guinalíu, M. (2008). Promoting consumer's participation in virtual brand communities: A new paradigm in branding strategy. *Journal of Marketing Communications, 14*(1), 19–36. https://doi.org/10.1080/13527260701535236

Choi, D., & Kim, J. (2004). Why people continue to play online games: In search of online contents. *Cyberpsychology & Behavior*, *7*(1), 11–25.

Csikszentmihalyi, M. (2008). *Flow: The psychology of optimal experience*. Harper Perennial Modern Classics.

Deterding, S., Dixon, D., Khaled, R., & Nacke, L. (2011). From game design elements to gamefulness. *Proceedings of the 15th International Academic MindTrek Conference on Envisioning Future Media Environments—MindTrek '11*, 9. https://doi.org/10.1145/2181037.2181040

Donaldson, T. (2020). Slow fashion artisan brands are leading the way to sustainable luxury. *WWD*. https://wwd.com/fashion-news/ready-to-wear/slow-fashion-artisan-luxury-sustainability-social-impact-1234575062/

Dopson, E. (2021). *What are virtual fitting rooms and how do they work? (2022)*. Shopify. https://www.shopify.co.uk/retail/virtual-fitting-rooms

Fortune Business Insights. (2020). *Virtual fitting room market size & share*. Global Report [2028]. https://www.fortunebusinessinsights.com/industry-reports/virtual-fitting-room-vfr-market-100322

Hootsuite. (2020). *Digital 2020*. https://www.hootsuite.com/resources/digital-2020

Huang, T.-L., & Liao, S.-L. (2017). Creating e-shopping multisensory flow experience through augmented-reality interactive technology. *Internet Research, 27*(2), 449–475. https://doi.org/10.1108/MRR-09-2015-0216

Huang, T. L., & Liu, F. H. (2014). Formation of augmented-reality interactive technology's persuasive effects from the perspective of experiential value. *Internet Research, 24*(1), 82–109. https://doi.org/10.1108/IntR-07-2012-0133

Hultén, B. (2011). Sensory marketing: The multi-sensory brand-experience concept. *European Business Review, 23*(3), 256–273. https://doi.org/10.1108/09555341111130245

Javornik, A. (2016). Augmented reality: Research agenda for studying the impact of its media characteristics on consumer behaviour. *Journal of Retailing and Consumer Services*. https://doi.org/10.1016/j.jretconser.2016.02.004

Jordan, D. (2021). *Why disabled people have been forgotten by the fashion industry*. Euronews. https://www.euronews.com/green/2021/02/13/why-disabled-people-have-been-forgotten-by-the-fashion-industry

Kannan, A. (2020). *Shopping for a beauty product? Try it on with Google*. https://blog.google/products/shopping/shopping-beauty-product-try-it-google/

Kohl's. (2020a). *Kohl's 2020 Fact Book*. https://corporate.kohls.com/content/dam/kohlscorp/investors/landing-page/Kohls%202020--Fact%20Book.pdf

Kohl's. (2020b). *Reimagining the digital shopping experience with Snapchat*. https://corporate.kohls.com/news/archive-/2020/august/reimagining-the-digital-shopping-experience-with-snapchat

Lee, D., Kim, H. S., & Kim, J. K. (2012). The role of self-construal in consumers' electronic word of mouth (eWOM) in social networking sites: A social cognitive approach. *Computers in Human Behavior, 28*(3), 1054–1062. http://www.sciencedirect.com/science/article/pii/S0747563212000118

Lee, H., & Xu, Y. (2020). Classification of virtual fitting room technologies in the fashion industry: From the perspective of consumer experience. *International Journal of Fashion Design, Technology and Education, 13*(1), 1–10. https://doi.org/10.1080/17543266.2019.1657505

Lee, J., Park, H., & Wise, K. (2013, September). Brand interactivity and its effects on the outcomes of advergame play. *New Media & Society*. https://doi.org/10.1177/1461444813504267

Luber, A. (2019). *Immersive branded experiences in YouTube and display ads*. https://www.blog.google/products/marketingplatform/360/immersive-branded-experiences-youtube-and-display-ads/

Merrilees, B., & Miller, D. (2019). Companion shopping: The influence on mall brand experiences. *Marketing Intelligence and Planning, 37*(4), 465–478. https://doi.org/10.1108/MIP-08-2018-0340

Muta, M., Ishikawa, Y., Yamanaka, T., & Masuko, S. (2018). Oz's fitting room: Fashion coordination support system by digital signage and human-driven virtual agent. *Proceedings of the 7th ACM International Symposium on Pervasive Displays*, 1–2. https://doi.org/10.1145/3205873.3210711

Papagiannis, H. (2018). Augmented human how technology is shaping the new reality. *Journal of Materials Processing Technology, 1*(1).

Polke, N., & Kumari, S. (2018). Avatar manager system for online fashion clothing APP. *2018 International Conference on Information, Communication, Engineering and Technology, ICICET 2018*, August, 1–4. https://doi.org/10.1109/ICICET.2018.8533812

Salazar, K. (2021). *Collaboration in the omnichannel experience*. https://www.nngroup.com/articles/omnichannel-collaboration/

Scholz, J., & Duffy, K. (2018). We ARe at home: How augmented reality reshapes mobile marketing and consumer-brand relationships. *Journal of Retailing and Consumer Services, 44*, 11–23. https://doi.org/10.1016/J.JRETCONSER.2018.05.004

Snap Inc. (2020). *Gucci*. Snapchat for Business. https://forbusiness.snapchat.com/inspiration/gucci-ar-tryon

Starbucks. (2016). *Discover the Pokémon GO Frappuccino at Starbucks*. https://stories.starbucks.com/stories/2016/starbucks-pokemon-go/

Statista Research Department. (2022). *Countries with most Snapchat users 2021*. Statista. https://www.statista.com/statistics/315405/snapchat-user-region-distribution/

Wanick, V., Ranchhod, A., & Gurau, C. (2017). Digital interactions and brand experience design: A future perspective. *Design Management Academy Conference 2017, 5*(2016), 1263–1281. https://doi.org/10.21606/dma.2017.129

Watson, A., Alexander, B., & Salavati, L. (2018). The impact of experiential augmented reality applications on fashion purchase. *International Journal of Retail & Distribution Management*. https://doi.org/10.1108/09574090910954864

WeThe15. (2021). *WeThe15: A global human rights movement for the 1.2 billion persons with disabilities*. https://www.wethe15.org/news/wethe15-a-global-human-rights-movement-for-the-12-billion-persons-with-disabilities

Wiggers, K. (2020). *Amazon's new AI technique lets users virtually try on outfits*. VentureBeat. https://venturebeat.com/2020/06/05/amazons-new-ai-technique-lets-users-virtually-try-on-outfits/

CHAPTER 5

Skins in the Game: Fashion Branding and Commercial Video Games

Emma Reay and Vanissa Wanick

Abstract The intersection between fashion branding and contemporary video games is a dynamic, rapidly evolving space. From luxury brands hosting runway shows in virtual environments to digital fashion collections designed exclusively for popular video game characters, these experimental crossovers are establishing new practices and setting new industry standards. In this chapter, we summarise some of the recent developments at this juncture and discuss the future implications both for the fashion industry and for the games industry. Using *Animal Crossing: New Horizons* (Nintendo, 2020) as case study, we explain how to use a commercial-off-the-shelf (COTS) video game to explore the nexus of gaming and fashion branding. We argue that in-game photography, customisable environments, simulated economies, interactive events, and

E. Reay (✉)
Anglia Ruskin University, Cambridge, UK
e-mail: E.J.Reay@soton.ac.uk

E. Reay · V. Wanick
Winchester School of Art, University of Southampton, Southampton, UK

E. Bazaki and V. Wanick (eds.), *Reinventing Fashion Retailing*, Palgrave Studies in Practice: Global Fashion Brand Management ,
https://doi.org/10.1007/978-3-031-11185-3_5

virtual design studios provide emerging creators with an entry point into design industries, as well as giving established brands a means to connect to new audiences. We suggest ways in which video games can be used in conjunction with social media platforms to foster creative self-expression and build networks. Specifically, we cover: (1) creating a cohesive aesthetic across a game's semiotic planes, (2) curating player experiences and ensuring access, (3) managing cross-channel promotion, and (4) encouraging playful engagement and the creation of user-generated content. We conclude by considering some of the ethical issues that arise from the commodification of play and the production of digital garments, including the markets that scaffold Non-Fungible Tokens (NFTs), the exploitation of fan labour, and legal questions of copyright.

Keywords Video games · Digital media · Virtual worlds · Metaverse · Non-fungible tokens

1 Introduction

The intersection between video games and luxury fashion brands is a rapidly evolving space. In recent years, a number of high-end fashion houses have entered the virtual worlds of contemporary games with a view to reaching new consumers and establishing future-oriented markets. Some of these first forays have taken the form of designing digital outfits known as 'skins' that can be purchased by players and worn by their avatars. In digital fashion, 'skins' are virtual masks that can be changed and afford customisation and personalisation, mostly related to avatar design (Palomo-Lovinski, 2008). Prada, for example, has collaborated with the multiplayer racing game *Riders Republic* to produce a digital sportswear line and a matching set of snowboards, skis, and BMX bikes that can be worn and used by avatars during online competitions. Similarly, Moschino has partnered with *The Sims* franchise to release physical and digital lines available to purchase in the real world or to download in the virtual world. This capsule collection playfully referenced the retro, pixelated graphics of 80s computer games, and the marketing copy invited consumers to 'become your own perfect avatar' (Scott, Instagram), suggesting that Moschino's designs allow one to customise one's real-world identity in a way that parallels the flexibility and freedom of character customisation in digital spaces. Balenciaga has followed suit by simultaneously launching physical and digital collections in partnership with the multiplayer, battle-royale game *Fortnite*. Other brands have produced physical garments inspired by popular videogames as a means of tapping into enthusiastic fan communities. Nike, for instance, has partnered with popular eSports game *League of Legends* to create footwear and apparel collections inspired by the game's aesthetics. They also released a line of footwear that features the PlayStation logo and colourway, allowing fans to express an aspect of their gamer identities through their apparel in the metaspace. Both Prada and Louis Vuitton have recruited virtual characters from the long-running *Final Fantasy* series to model physical garments and accessories. Louis Vuitton, for example, had the pink-haired heroine, Lightning, from *Final Fantasy XIII* wield their handbags like weapons and wear their leather jackets like armour in an advertising campaign launched in 2016. Louis Vuitton also marked the 200-year birthday of brand's founder by releasing a mobile game entitled *Louis: The Game*. This third-person adventure game allows players to direct a neotonised, wooden avatar with a face framed by flower petals through a series of whimsical meadows and charming forests, collecting two-hundred birthday candles along their way. These candles unlock a set of nostalgic postcards that provide autobiographical details about Louis' life. Marking an important anniversary of the historic fashion house with a mobile game fuses tradition with contemporary technology, implying that Louis Vuitton's style is timeless and can survive endless remediations.

Balenciaga has also created an original video game to promote their brand, designing an entire virtual world in which to host their Fall 2021 runway show. This bespoke digital experience was entitled *Afterworld: The Age of Tomorrow* (Dimension Studio, 2020), a name that acknowledges the brand's future orientation with regard to the nexus of fashion and entertainment technology, as well as the apocalyptic motifs threaded through the collection. An in-person runway show would have been almost impossible due to the travel restrictions and social distancing rules necessary to respond to a global pandemic, but Balenciaga's virtual experience provided an effective alternative. In addition to giving guests the opportunity to view the season's collection up close and in high definition, the photorealistic 3D environments and first-person movement mechanics allowed Balenciaga to curate a memorable, immersive adventure.

Players of *Afterworld: The Age of Tomorrow* embark on an intriguing and somewhat uneasy journey through moody, post-apocalyptic zones, culminating in an enchanted wood with an epic, Neo-Medieval feel. The soundscape changes with the environment from the minimalist, dissonant, synthetic melodies of a whirring and grinding Brutalist city to birdsong and orchestral strings as the sun rises over a mountainous forest. The surreal, virtual world is populated by stylish non-player characters (NPCs), dressed head-to-toe in Balenciaga. The combination of their hyperrealism and their vacant non-responsiveness to the player's presence has an uncanny effect, but rather than breaking immersion, their *cyborgian* aloofness establishes these NPCs as living works of art. Furthermore, it emphasises the communicative power of their outfits. The streamlined, simple mechanics are limited to being guided through the game's spaces by neon arrows. The lack of more layered interactions shapes an experience in which 'seeing' is the active verb, aligning the game with the experience of visiting a gallery. At the game's conclusion, the first-person perspective shifts to a third-person perspective as the player's avatar—dressed in a cyberpunk suit of armour—takes her place at the mountain's highest peak. 'Seeing' expands to 'being seen' as the strikingly dressed avatar adopts a power stance in front of an impressive landscape, thereby mirroring the 'seeing'/'being seen' oscillation that characterises the experience of attending a luxury runway show.

Whereas Balenciaga developed an entire virtual world to showcase their designs, other brands have constructed unique spaces within existing video games. Gucci, for example, has created a surreal garden inside *Roblox* that players can visit online. Since *Roblox* is a game creation platform that specifically targets young game designers aged between eleven and eighteen, it could be surmised that Gucci is attempting to court a new generation of consumers who may not otherwise encounter the brand through traditional media channels. Other designers—from Anna Sui to Isabel Marant to Marc Jacobs—have built themed islands in *Animal Crossing: New Horizons (AC:NH)* as imaginative locales in which fans can engage with the brand. It is the latter game that we will use in this chapter to illustrate the branding opportunities afforded by contemporary digital games.

We have chosen *AC:NH* specifically because it has extremely simple, accessible mechanics and a short learning-curve, whilst still granting players a meaningful degree of creative agency. That is to say, unlike Balenciaga's virtual world—which required a team of technically skilled people, a large budget, and a significant amount of time to create—virtual worlds built in *AC:NH* are comparatively easy to design and implement. The fact that large, established brands with experienced marketing teams and new, emerging brands managed by one or two individuals both have access to the same set of creative, marketing tools in *AC:NH* democratises the process in a way that we find ethically complex and relevant to ongoing discussions about the commercialisation and monetisation of the 'Metaverse'. Furthermore, it is significant that fashion designs in *AC:NH* are free to download. There are many video games that sell skins and other cosmetic features, but in *AC:NH* clothes and accessories cannot be purchased with 'real' currencies within the game. That is not to say that markets do not exist outside of the game that involve the exchange of 'real' currencies for in-game items, but that this is not supported within the trading and gifting mechanisms of the game. In the next section, we outline the main theoretical debates around fashion and games in general. This is followed by an in-depth case study of *AC:NH*.

2 Background: Fashion, Games, and Consumer Behaviour

In this section, we outline the seven components that summarise the relationship between fashion games and consumer behaviour: (1) self-identity; (2) self-discovery; (3) self-expression; (4) status; (5) digital garments; (6) artistic value; and (7) brand interactivity (see Fig. 1). Within the seven components, three are related to the construct of the 'self', which can be mostly attached to digital 'self-image' or, in other words, the players' avatars or characters.

Victoria Tran (2019) has argued that fashion in video games is key to expressing character attributes and conveying narrative information. She concludes that players expect the outfits of NPCs to be meaningful and legible. Concurrently, the visuals and aesthetic possibilities that games provide can evoke a sense of identity since players can choose their character appearance, styles, and skins (Kim et al., 2012). According to Kim et al. (2012), characters are virtual representations of the players and can be chosen by their attractiveness, vividness, design, and the role that they play in the game. In this particular case, Kim et al. (2012) studied the fashion of characters in an MMORPG, which has the role-playing aspect

Fig. 1 The relationship between fashion, games, and consumer behaviour (*Source* The authors)

as a core mechanic; thus, choosing a character is a key component in this type of game.

Since fashion can evoke one's idea of self-concept and it extends the self by clothing and accessories (Loussaïef et al., 2019), it is possible that game 'skins' might evoke such perception, since character choice allows players to express their identities (Kim et al., 2012). Due to the idea of ownership, self-image and self-presentation, this sense of the self can be enhanced and defined by people's fashion possessions, which is extended to the digital realm. This might represent a sense of status. Self-expression through digital fashion is complex due to the many combinations that arise, from choosing different body types, eye colours, skin colours, and outfits (Liao, 2011). For some people, the process of choosing a style and changing outfits in virtual worlds can be extremely engaging and playful.

Dressing up allows people to communicate their values with others, and within that, people can also communicate status and identity (Palomo-Lovinski, 2008). In addition, choosing an avatar in the digital world would also imply that that avatar is part of the virtual world's society (Makryniotis, 2018).

Makryniotis (2018) argues that games offer many opportunities for fashion design as the actual garment 'fit' is not as important as colours and texture, for example. This suggests that the function of fashion in digital worlds is mostly related to self-representation and identity. The digital garment might also reflect the materiality of the digital itself, such as 3D simulations, fabric textures, and dynamic garments (e.g., animated colours and patterns) that includes the programmatic element of digital dressing (K. H. Choi, 2022).

In virtual worlds, players tend to create a version of themselves that doesn't have to be exactly similar to their 'real-life' self; these are symbolic representations of their desired self and can drive them into a journey of self-discovery (Loker et al., 2008). Although this can sound like a fantastic version of the self, some virtual worlds and games can bring the value 'dressing' has in the real world. This is because some games have their own economy and online designers have discovered that they can sell digital garments online (Loker et al., 2008). By doing so, there is a new purpose of value that is added to the mix. Whereas technology can allow customisation, self-expression and communication of one's ideals (Palomo-Lovinski, 2008), it is not very clear how the addition of the financial component reflects inequalities from the real world.

The integration of brands and games can take many forms. Brands can appear in the game, particularly in the background as a product placement. In this case, the game is not designed around the brand, and its appearance functions as product placement. On the other hand, there are games designed around a brand (i.e., initially termed 'advergames') and these games provide a rhetorical response towards the brand message.

Research suggests that when games are designed around a brand or have a high level of alignment with the branded content, players might recall the brand more easily (Peters & Leshner, 2013; Shelton & Gross, 2010; Winkler & Buckner, 2006). However, a negative experience with the game still prevails and erases any possible positive attitude towards the brand. Thus, a bad experience with the game evokes a bad experience with the brand. This might be that one of the reasons current collaborations between fashion brands and commercial video games are on the rise.

One, the game itself has already a fan base and players; and two, fashion brands only need to design the skins needed to dress the avatars, which means that the costs can be lower than creating a full game from scratch that is not engaging or fun. Considering this, three exploratory research questions arise:

- How do fashion brands manifest in commercial video games?
- How do players respond to these manifestations?
- What are the implications of the use of sponsored 'skins' within commercial video games?

In order to address and illustrate these questions, we will provide contextual information about *AC:NH* and a detailed outline of the game's mechanics that pertain to fashion design and the buying and selling of digital garments. This is explained in the next section.

3 Case Study: Animal Crossing: New Horizons

In March 2020, at the beginning of the COVID-19 pandemic, Nintendo released *Animal Crossing: New Horizons:* a real-time 'island-living' simulator for the Switch. In its first month, it broke the record for most digital units sold for a console game, and as of June 2021, it has sold over 33.89 million copies worldwide (Nintendo, 2021). During a period of social isolation, disruption, and uncertainty, *AC:NH* provided players with a refuge of predictable rhythms, charming art style, and wholesome social encounters. In its virtual locations, players celebrated weddings, birthdays, graduations, and other important events that had been cancelled in the physical world. They found comfort in establishing daily routines and working towards simple goals and, most importantly for this chapter, they found an outlet for their creativity.

AC:NH encourages creative self-expression in several ways. Players can engage in town-planning, and are tasked with designing the island's infrastructure, communal spaces, and the layout of the villagers' houses. They can choose the appearance of their own house and design its interior using furniture and decorations purchased using 'bells'—the in-game currency—from the island's shop, along with floors and wallpaper procured from a cute nomadic camel. Bells are earned by selling natural resources harvested from the island or items crafted using those resources to the twin tanuki pups who run the local shop 'Nook's Cranny', named after the island's affable landlord, Tom Nook. Once players have reached a certain level, they can also terraform the island, adding cliffs, waterfalls, lakes, and rivers.

In addition to customising the environment, players can also customise the appearance of their avatar—from its hairstyle, skin tone, and facial features, to its outfits, emotes, and accessories. Items of clothing can be bought from the island's hedgehog-run tailor shop, acquired from other players via the internet, or they can be designed by players using simple templates. As with the island's other amenities, the tailor's shop does not materialise until the player has reached certain goals. They must first build the island's general store and the island's museum that hosts the collections of insects and fish the player can catch using a net and a fishing line. On the one hand, the fact that players can choose whether to sell their specimens to Nook's Cranny for bells or donate them to the museum to be housed in a peaceful, public aquarium and insectarium suggests that the game values individual wealth and social service equally. This primes players to see sharing fashion designs with each other free of charge as a valid and integral part of the in-game garment economy. On the other hand, the fact that the tailor's shop is only available to players who have invested a significant amount of time in the game suggests that clothing is a status symbol in the world of *Animal Crossing*. That is to say, an increase in consumer options and purchasing power is still tied to the 'meritocratic' capitalist rhetoric of video game grind.

After the conditions pertaining to the museum and the general store are met, a blue hedgehog named Mabel will appear sporadically on the island with a pop-up shop selling clothes. If the player interacts with her a sufficient number of times—and spends an undisclosed sum of bells on her wares—she then announces that she would like to set up a permanent business on the island, and tasks the player with finding her a suitable plot of land. Again, the player's induction to the buying and selling of virtual clothes is predicated on a neighbourly act of service. Mabel opens her shop alongside her introverted sister, Sable, who is always found diligently and tirelessly sewing new garments in the shop. Once the hedgehogs are settled in, the player can use the terminal at the back of her shop to share their fashion designs online with other players.

Another key player in the game's simulated fashion market is a third hedgehog sister, Label. Label is an aspiring high-end designer who sets the player a series of challenges to help inspire her own creativity.

These challenges involve Label suggesting a category to the player (e.g., 'formal', 'vacation', or 'sporty') who must then return dressed in an appropriate outfit. The player's reward from Label varies according to how many of the clothing items that they choose match the brief. The best outfits receive an item from Label's own clothing line, 'Labelle'. These challenges not only motivate the player to invest in a wide range of clothing items, but also encourage the player to think carefully about how they coordinate different aspects of their avatar's appearance.

AC:NH features an in-game camera so that players can capture and display their fashion creations and outfit ensembles. These photographs can be carefully posed, and players are invited to consider the aesthetic effects of lighting, backdrops, and props. In this sense, players act as photographers, models, fashion designers, and location managers to manifest their creative vision. What is more, *AC:NH* enables players share their images online with other players across a variety of social media platforms. There are hundreds of Facebook groups, Instagram accounts, Discord servers, blogs, and Twitter accounts dedicated to the *Animal Crossing* franchise. Some are established and moderated by Nintendo's marketing team (e.g., the Twitter account @animalcrossing, which shares the latest *Animal Crossing* news through the persona of 'Isabelle', an anthropomorphic dog who works as the avatar's in-game assistant). The majority, however, are community-run. The primary purposes of these groups are to trade items, to manipulate the 'stalk' market (an in-game stock market that involves the buying and selling of turnips), and to share player-created scenes and designs.

The game world itself is also an online social platform, in that individuals can host up to eight other players on their islands. Each player's island can be accessed using a unique code and during visits other players can give each other gifts, explore the customised environments, and participate in minigames. These in-built social affordances can be used to engage consumers in playful and personal interactions with a brand. On Net-a-Porter's island, for example, players are welcomed as guests and invited to admire the island's features, to claim exclusive items, and to interact with other visitors. The virtual spaces are designed to evoke a relaxing, indulgent getaway (e.g., 'Beach Relaxation', 'Spa Area', 'Hot Spring Bath', 'Gym and Mediation'), whilst also showcasing a consistent brand image reinforced through the use of recognisable Net-a-Porter monochromatic colour palettes and iconic patterns. Net-a-Porter's island was created by brand consultant *WeSuperSeed* and inspired by Net-a-Porter's brand identity and their London headquarters. When visiting the island, players are encouraged not just to sight-see but to *be seen*: the environment functions as extensive backdrop for posed shareable screenshots that document one's presence at an exclusive event.

Digital interactions with customers on branded islands can exceed the straightforward exchanges that take place in online shops, which often feel impersonal, anonymous, and purely transactional. Whilst items of clothing are still central to the appeal of these digital spaces, brands can use the full range of customisation tools available to create a wholistic, multidimensional representation of their aesthetic. Significantly, online visitors can engage playfully with this aesthetic by incorporating it into their own creative expression. Unlike in most physical spaces, within the world of *AC:NH*, everyone has access to a common set of design tools and processes. This creates a sense of equality between the brand and the players: it dissolves the traditional binary of producers and consumers, positioning all participants as creators.

This dissolution of boundaries is also a central part of the staging of Net-a-Porter's digital runway. Whilst most catwalks privilege a certain type of body, digital avatars in *AC:NH* cannot be ranked and categorised using the same set of exclusionary standards. Any player can don an outfit and take their place on the runway, and—although some emotes take time to unlock—all players have access to the same walk animations and the same set of poses. Finally, there is a joyful and almost irreverent humour to translating high fashion, luxury items into skins that fit a dumpy, neotonised, squishy avatar. The 'dress-up game' genre has a long history, but recent iterations in the mobile gaming space such as *Drest* (Lucy Yeomans, 2019) fill the gap left by the dwindling of glossy, print magazines with an innovative, interactive alternative. *Drest* combines elements of social media platforms, competitive gameplay, and high-end digital fashion catalogues to scaffold an experience that works both as sales tool and as a pastime. The user interface of *Drest* is elegant and refined, suggesting that it targets a mature and sophisticated player. *AC:NH*, in contrast, casts a wider net to encompass those for whom being 'fashion-forward' is only one pillar of their identity.

We will now discuss two specific examples of players and brands using *AC:NH* to design and promote fashion. In the first case study, we look at how photographer Kara Chung used Instagram to build a cross-over audience of gamers and designers, and her consequent collaboration with luxury fashion brands. In the second case study, we examine how jewellery brand Pandora created a 'Dream Island' to tie the products to a particular lifestyle and identity.

4 Kara Chung: Animal Crossing Fashion Archive

Kara Chung is a visual artist, photographer, and gamer who started playing *AC:NH* during the COVID-19 pandemic. She created an Instagram account (@animalcrossingfashionarchive) as a means of sharing her outfit designs with friends and family. What began as a private project for a small, personal audience became a social media sensation, attracting 37,000 followers as of November 2021, coverage by fashion news outlets such as Vogue, and brand partnerships with international, luxury fashion houses. In collaboration with Reference Festival, a Berlin-based fashion organisation, Chung is credited with organising one of the first runway shows to be held in *AC:NH.*

The challenge that Chung identifies in using *AC:NH* as a fashion design tool is 'distilling' the essence of a brand. Garment designs must be simplified in order to be mapped onto the in-game templates. This means that colourways and patterns take precedent over texture or cuts. The game's fashion customisation tools are fairly limited, and the resultant designs are simple and highly stylised. These restrictions arguably invite creative workarounds: they require players to identify and preserve the defining features of a garment, which in turn serves to hone their critical eye when viewing their own work and the work of other designers. Furthermore, these limitations mean that creators must reach for other communicative devices to express their ideas, which in *AC:NH* means staging, lighting, furniture, and props. Finally, one can see the limited set of design tools as being vital for the 'lusory attitude' players are invited to take towards the designing of apparel. Many play theorists and games scholars including Bernard Suits (1978/2020), Johann Huizinga (1948/2016), and Jesper Juul (2005) have asserted that the act of play is best characterised as the voluntary attempt to overcome unnecessary obstacles. That is to say, the rules of many games prohibit the most efficient route to achieving a game's victory—in golf, for example, the rules do not allow players to simply pick up the ball with their hands in order to place it into the hole. The pleasure of play can be found in working within and around a set of rules—diligently mastering them or ingeniously hacking them—in order to enjoy the satisfaction of achieving a goal. We can see a parallel between this definition of play and the pleasurable challenge of remediating a luxury, designer item using a restricted toolset. In other words, we consider the digital resourcefulness showcased in adapting high fashion designs in *AC:NH* to be a form of creativity and a sign of playfulness.

Chung astutely notes in an interview (High Snobiety, 2020) that fashion in *AC:NH* has less in common with browsing clothes a physical shop and more in common with flicking through the pages of a print magazine. This comparison draws attention to the fact that there are multiple ways to participate in high fashion beyond simply owning a particular garment. Games such as *AC:NH* facilitate a practice not dissimilar to creating a physical scrapbook with images cut out of magazines. In this sense, *AC:NH* allows fashion fans to align their identities with particular brands in (virtual) public spaces without having to purchase expensive items. Furthermore, fans can show their admiration for a brand whilst simultaneously showing off their own creative flair in their remediation of a garment. That is to say, *AC:NH* designs pay homage to their brand inspirations.

Chung's skill at remediating designer looks continues to attract the attention of luxury brands, who have commissioned her to create digital versions of their garments in *AC:NH* and then share these designs with her followers. This kind of grassroots marketing approach is an underexplored facet of the now ubiquitous 'influencer culture'.

5 Pandora Island

An update to *AC:NH* in July 2020 introduced a feature called 'Dream Addresses' that allows players to visit other people's islands even when the person they are visiting is not online. Dream Addresses are unique twelve-digit codes that can be shared online. Unlike hosting a particular event on an island at a set time, the Dream Address functionality means players can explore a specific island whenever they like. Since these visits are framed as 'dreams', players cannot bring items to the island, nor can they alter or damage the island in any way. This update provides brands with the opportunity to curate a pervasive virtual that requires little upkeep or surveillance after its initial launch. The following discussion will analyse the Dream Address created by the jewellery brand Pandora. It will look specifically at how Pandora creates a consistent aesthetic across multiple semiotic planes, how the brand has used ludic devices to shape a particular player experience, and how the island encourages player-created content and the organic dissemination of the brand's logo across social platforms.

When the player initially wakes up on Pandora's island, they find themselves on the plaza directly next to the custom design catalogue station. This is a prompt to browse and download the Pandora-themed garment designs, which can be worn immediately. These free designs not only provide an incentive for players to visit Pandora Island, but also serve to create a sense of belonging for players during their visit. The island is designed to evoke the experience of attending an exclusive press event. The customisable houses are styled as 'The Studio', 'The Green Room', 'The Selfie Space', and 'The Dance Floor'. The outdoor environments include an arcade, a spa area, a diner, and a nature park. The choice of locales and decorations create a luxurious, opulent feel but the inclusion of certain kitsch items—for example, the pink garden flamingo statues—ensure the atmosphere stays accessible and relaxed. Furthermore, the island is not overly manicured and there are a few weeds. Items and lighting are used throughout the island to iterate on a soft pink and purple colour scheme. Posters are placed around the island's venues, proclaiming one-word slogans such as 'Blessed', 'Peace', and 'Believe'. The overall aesthetic is best characterised as cool femininity.

There are numerous locations around the island that function as backdrops for photoshoots. The brand's logo can be seen on the island's flag, as well as on customised floor tiles that demarcate a dance floor, meaning that any dissemination of player-creator screenshots on social media will also disseminate the brand name. The brand positions itself as generous by providing players with gifts of sparklers, party poppers, and balloons. This creates goodwill between the brand and potential consumers. Although Pandora's Dream Island establishes the brand's identity across a number of semiotic levels, we feel it could have gone one step further to create consonance across the ludic plane too. The brand is known for its iconic charm bracelets, for example, which are designed to mark significant life events. The island could have made the most of this 'collector's mentality' by designing a scavenger hunt around the island for themed items, for example.

6 Further Thoughts

In this concluding section, we will reflect on some of the potential positive and negative effects of combining fashion branding and digital games. One issue is the gamification of consumerism, wherein 'consumerism' is defined as a social and economic order that encourages the acquisition of goods in ever-increasing amounts. Games scholars have examined how ideologies of capitalism and consumption are expressed in the *Animal Crossing* series. Critics such as Ian Bogost (2007), Emma Vossen (2020), and Naomi Clark (2020) explore the tensions inherent in the franchise between eco-pastoralism and capitalist growth, analysing in-game economies and resource management systems. Using a platform like *AC:NH* to sell real-world products could be seen to rupture the 'magic circle' of play (Tekinbaş & Zimmerman, 2005) and undermine the escapist fantasy of being able to exist in a space free from the negative effects of late-stage capitalism. On the other hand, one could argue that playful simulations of real-world economic systems have radical potential to draw attention to collective consumption habits that would otherwise be made invisible through a process of naturalisation.

One positive effect of the digitisation of fashion could be a movement towards greater inclusion in terms of body type and gender, as players can experiment with all aspects of their avatars' appearances. *AC:NH* specifically designates 'gender' as 'style', and allows players to change their 'style' at any point in the game. The player's chosen gender/style is in fact, mostly irrelevant as other characters refer to the player in the second person or using 'they/them' pronouns, and all hairstyles/facial features are available irrespective of the 'style' one chooses. Liberated from social constructions that are predicated on anatomical features, players may find fashion to be more inclusive, welcoming, and freeing. That said, games scholars such as Lisa Nakamura (2002) and Kishonna Gray (2020) warn against naïve enthusiasm about the post-body age promised by digital tools for self-creation. Using a range of methodologies, both researchers have shown that racism, ableism, and heterosexism invariably persist in virtual spaces.

The entwining of digital games and fashion branding may create new job roles. Game development studios could consider adding a fashion designer to the team. As mentioned by Makryniotis (2018), not many fashion designers are employed by the games industry. This opens new possibilities for interdisciplinary games design roles, similar to what happens in the filmmaking industry (e.g., costume design).

It is possible that digital fashion may propose an environmental-friendly alternative to traditional clothing. *DressX*, a digital wardrobe where you can pay for outfits that defy the laws of physics and/or the constraints of the human body positions itself as a green alternative to the extremely wasteful and resource-intensive production processes of the fashion industry. According to the *DressX* website, digital garment production emits 97% less than a physical garment. The app allows users to superimpose items over photographs of themselves, which can then be shared on social media platforms and dating apps. *DressX* can also be used in combination with *Roblox* and it features different fashion designers (with different price tags attached to the digital garments). However, this business model might be masking a more serious problem. In fact, many luxury brands have been implementing sustainability as a marketing strategy, under the umbrella of greenwashing, with the aim to gain public trust (Akrout & Guercini, 2022).

The digital gaming space is currently reckoning with the implications of online markets that trade in cryptocurrencies and non-fungible tokens (NFTs), which are digital assets that can be sold and bought online and are attached to a single digital signature. Points of contention include the negative environmental impact of energy-intensive blockchain mining, money laundering, pyramid schemes, and security breaches through hacking or human error. Furthermore, many experienced game designers have publicly emphasised that the idea of interoperable digital skins and accessories that can be transferred between games is neither feasible nor desirable (Gilbert, 2022).

Another issue to mention is the exploitation of fan labour. Henry Jenkins (1992) has compared fan labour to craftwork and community-led folk production. One could argue that big, multinational fashion corporations are exploiting the free circulation of creative endeavours that emerge organically on *AC:NH* in order to assimilate this energy back into capitalist structures. This raises the question of whether genuine consumer co-creation can take place when there is such an unequal power balance between brand and fan. Framing unpaid labour as a 'hobby' makes it difficult to value the necessary skills required to make digital creations and to ensure credit and ownership are allocated appropriately. Fans find intrinsic value in acts of creative customisation, but this could shift to digital play experiences to being one extrinsically motivated by default (e.g., creating online engagement in order to boost a brand and sell a product or earn a financial incentive out of it).

Finally, it is important to apply lessons learned in the physical space to the digital space. Consider that high fashion has always stolen from the streets but subsequently added an exorbitant price tag, how equal, then, are these so-called 'partnerships' between fashion brands and creative players? And to what extent can we see the incursion of big-name brands into play spaces as a form of digital gentrification?

References

Akrout, H., & Guercini, S. (2022). Sustainability in fashion and luxury marketing: Results, paradoxes and potentialities. *Journal of Global Fashion Marketing, 13*(2), 91–100. https://doi.org/10.1080/20932685.2021.2017320

Bogost, I. (2007). *Persuasive games: The expressive power of videogames*. The MIT Press

Choi, K. H. (2022). 3D dynamic fashion design development using digital technology and its potential in online platforms. *Fashion and Textiles, 9*(1), 1–28. https://doi.org/10.1186/S40691-021-00286-1/TABLES/3

Clark, N. (2020). *Why tom nook symbolises village debt in 18th century Japan*. YouTube, https://www.youtube.com/watch?v=BgEmbXPZX4s

Dimension Studio. (2020). *Afterworld: The age of tomorrow*. Dimension Studio.

Gilbert, B. (2022). *Video game makers explain why a main 'metaverse' promise is false*. https://www.businessinsider.com/video-game-makers-explain-why-main-metaverse-promise-is-false-2022-1?r=US&IR=T

Gray, K. (2020). *Intersectional tech: Black users in digital gaming*.

Huizinga, J. (1948/2016). *Homo ludens: A study of the play-element in culture*. Angelica Press.

Jenkins, H. (1992). Textual poachers: Television fans and participatory culture (studies in culture and communication). In *Les cultes médiatiques*.

Juul, J. (2005). *Half-real: Video games between real rules and fictional worlds*. MIT.

Kim, S. J., Kim, K. H., & Mattila, P. (2012). The role of fashion in the characters of online games. *Journal of Global Fashion Marketing, 3*(2), 81–88. https://doi.org/10.1080/20932685.2012.10593110

Liao, C. (2011). *Virtual fashion play as embodied identity re/assembling: Second life fashion bloggers and their avatar bodies* (pp. 101–127). https://doi.org/10.1007/978-0-85729-361-9_6

Loker, S., Ashdown, S., & Carnrite, E. (2008). Dress in the third dimension. *Clothing and Textiles Research Journal, 26*(2), 164–176. https://doi.org/10.1177/0887302X08315176

Loussaïef, L., Ulrich, I., & Damay, C. (2019). How does access to luxury fashion challenge self-identity? Exploring women's practices of joint and non-ownership. *Journal of Business Research, 102*, 263–272. https://doi.org/10.1016/J.JBUSRES.2019.02.020

Makryniotis, T. (2018). Fashion and costume design in electronic entertainment—Bridging the gap between character and fashion design. *Fashion Practice, 10*(1), 99–118. https://doi.org/10.1080/17569370.2017.1412595
Nakamura, L. (2002). *Cybertypes: Race, ethnicity, and identity on the internet*.
Nintendo. (2020). *Animal crossing: New horizons*. Nintendo
Nintendo. (2021). *Nintendo sales data*. Retrieved https://www.nintendo.co.jp/ir/en/finance/hard_soft/
Palomo-Lovinski, N. (2008). Extensible dress: The future of digital clothing. *Clothing and Textiles Research Journal*, *26*(2). https://doi.org/10.1177/0887302X07310078
Peters, S., & Leshner, G. (2013). Get in the game: The effects of game-product congruity and product placement proximity on game players' processing of brands embedded in advergames. *Journal of Advertising, 42*(2–3), 113–130. https://doi.org/10.1080/00913367.2013.774584
Shelton, A., & Gross, M. L. (2010). Advergames and the effects of game-product congruity. *Computers in Human Behavior, 26*(6), 1259–1265. http://www.sciencedirect.com/science/article/pii/S0747563210000804
Suits, B. (1978/2020). *The grasshopper: Games, life and utopia*. Heritage.
Tekinbaş, K. S., & Zimmerman, E. (2005). *Rules of play: Game design fundamentals*.
Tran, V. (2019). Why fashion in (most) games sucks, and why you should care. *GDC*, YouTube https://www.youtube.com/watch?v=Pr7rzcwOz_g
Vossen, E. (2020). Tom nook, capitalist or comrade? *Loading, 13*(22), 109–134.
Winkler, T., & Buckner, K. (2006). Receptiveness of gamers to embedded brand messages in advergames: Attitudes towards product placement. *Journal of Interactive Advertising, 7*, 37–46.

CHAPTER 6

Becoming a Fashion Blogger Entrepreneur: The Case of Chiara Ferragni

Eirini Bazaki and Elena Cedrola

Abstract The increasing presence of social media and digital technology in consumers' lives has changed the way fashion brands work and communicate with their customers. In a consumer-driven market, a new genre of marketing has been created, where influencers and fashion bloggers act as mediators in the relationship between the customer and the brand. Bloggers gain more power as intermediaries than fashion brands have directly to influence consumers. Therefore, fashion companies seek to collaborate with bloggers to co-create and promote their products and set trends for the future. From a fashion consumer's perspective, blogging is increasingly seen as an opportunity to join the fashion industry and build a personal brand. This chapter focuses on Chiara Ferragni, a successful fashion blogger and entrepreneur who started her career as a

E. Bazaki (✉)
Winchester School of Art, University of Southampton, Southampton, UK
e-mail: E.Bazaki@soton.ac.uk

E. Cedrola
University of Macerata, Macerata, Italy

E. Bazaki and V. Wanick (eds.), *Reinventing Fashion Retailing*, Palgrave Studies in Practice: Global Fashion Brand Management ,
https://doi.org/10.1007/978-3-031-11185-3_6

fashion amateur and is now a fashion empress. Indeed, 13 years since it was launched, Ferragni's blog has more than 27,2 million followers today through Instagram and has evolved into a successful lifestyle magazine. The brand Chiara Ferragni, which launched in 2013 as a fashion shoe brand, has now successfully extended to several other product categories including clothes, accessories and jewellery, leading a new fast-growing sector of fashion blogger entrepreneur brands. This chapter explores how Ferragni was able to disrupt the traditional model of the fashion industry and become an integral part of it. The chapter examines the essential skills, strategies and capital that enabled Ferragni to transform from a fashion amateur to a fashion icon and a successful fashion entrepreneur.

Keywords Entrepreneurship · Blogging · Chiara Ferragni · Personal branding techniques · Fashion · Authenticity · Influencer marketing

1 Introduction

The pervasiveness of social media and digital technology in the consumer-driven market has enabled personal fashion blogs to become an integral part of most prestigious fashion brand strategies, i.e., advertising through sponsored posts, brand endorsements and developing co-branding products (Delisle & Parmentier, 2016). In the modern world, fashion blogs serve as a means of expression, where bloggers can visually document their personal style (Pedroni, 2015). When posting photos, some bloggers stand out owing to their distinctive styles. One such example is the famous fashion blogger Chiara Ferragni with her blog "The Blonde Salad". Ferragni started her blog as an ordinary consumer and in just a few years, she became a global brand managing a €40 million assets (Buffolo, 2021).

Marketing scholars have taken a key interest in conceptualising what triggers the success of fashion bloggers, including their motivations, strategies and tactics (Delisle & Parmentier, 2016), physical characteristics, market characteristics, leadership skills and business acumen. Yet, despite the popularity of this phenomenon, previous research has found that most fashion bloggers fail in their attempts to build their own personal brand (Pedroni, 2015). Self-branding is considered mandatory for the development of a successful online presence. Examples of strong personal brands are found across different sectors, some of the most notable examples in the sports industry include David Beckham, Cristiano Ronaldo (Parmentier & Fischer, 2012), in the fashion industry Giorgio Armani, Dona Karan, Victoria Beckham, (Parmentier et al., 2013) and in the entertainment industry Alexa Chung, Hilary Devey.

To further our understanding of how bloggers succeed in creating strong personal brands, this chapter considers dimensions previously suggested in the literature alongside an analysis of Chiara Ferragni as a case study. The aim is to provide a roadmap for building and maintaining a successful fashion blog. This chapter answers three main questions: (a) How accessible is the entrepreneurial blogosphere to ordinary consumers? (b) What resources do ordinary consumers need to become successful fashion entrepreneurs in the blogosphere? (c) What are the key strategic steps in becoming a successful fashion entrepreneur in the blogosphere? It is one of the first studies on this topic to unveil the process of building and growing a fashion blog form a personal blog to a business. This chapter calls to attention the essential, peripheral and complimentary skills for building and maintaining a fashion blog and the underlying theories involved. It also offers recommendations to ordinary consumers who consider blogging a career opportunity and fashion bloggers who seek to understand which practices will lead to their success in the fashion blogosphere.

2 Literature Review

This literature review explores the current state of knowledge concerning the resources and processes of becoming a fashion blogger entrepreneur, with particular reference to taste as a distinctive identifier, the value of authenticity in leadership (its dimensions and meanings), blog development stages, skills required and entrepreneurial mindset characteristics that set fashion blogger entrepreneurs aside from ordinary consumers.

3 Taste as a Resource

> Taste classifies, and it classifies the classifier. Social subjects, classified by their classifications, distinguish themselves by the distinctions they make. (1984, Bourdieu's, p. 6 in McQuarrie et al., 2013, p. 139)

In line with in Gronow's (1997) work on the sociology of taste, the latter is defined as an individual's capacity to apply aesthetic judgement and skill to discriminate between beautiful and graceful versus the elaborated and unappealing (McQuarrie et al., 2013). Taste has levels and individuals can be assessed on their ability to exercise taste (McQuarrie et al., 2013). Taste is reinforced with cultural capital. Following Bourdieu's more recent work on the dynamic formulation of cultural capital, fashion bloggers can enhance their cultural capital through repeat exercise and display of taste (McQuarrie et al., 2013). Taste can be used to draw boundaries between those who share the same taste and those who don't. Taste can be used to create groups and bring people together, but also foster solidarity and distinction among its prime members (McQuarrie et al., 2013). Taste can be used as a resource for personal branding.

4 Taste Leadership—The Battle for Authenticity

Marketers have long recognised the importance of authenticity as an attribute (Audrezet et al., 2020). Authenticity improved message receptivity, perceived quality, consumers purchase intentions and increases overall desire for lifestyle brands and products (Audrezet et al., 2020; Duffy, 2013, Marwick, 2013). Although the concept of authenticity broadly revolves around the notions of what is true, genuine and real, there is widespread agreement that authenticity is socially constructed based on what is observed and rather than the innate characteristics of an object (Beverland & Farrelly, 2010). In the online context, a number of studies have studied the techniques used to present an authentic self (Duffy, 2013; Marwick, 2013; Savignac et al., 2012; Shifman, 2018). For example, Savignac et al. (2012) in their study of opinion leaders' authenticity management in a streetwear community found that adopting an informal tone, contextualising in detail the subjects of their blog entries, publishing blog entries that reflected their offline reality were instrumental in the construction of an authentic self. Marwick (2013) work on celebrity self, interprets the relationship between the blogger and its followers as the relationship that celebrities have with their fans.

Going beyond self-representation, in a more recent study Audrezet et al. (2020), found support for two authenticity strategies deliberately used by SMEs to guide their brand partnerships, passionate authenticity and transparent authenticity. Passionate authenticity entails an inner, genuine desire of a person or a brand to communicate their passion to a broader audience while transparent authenticity relates to disclosing information about contracts, agreements and partnerships with particular brands. The two authenticity strategies bridge the gap between personal branding techniques that aim to promote individuals' transparent authenticity and self-determination theory that conceptualises passion as solely an intrinsic as opposed to extrinsic motivation (Audrezet et al., 2020).

In his work on symbols of a class status, Goffman (1951) distinguishes between taste preference and taste leadership. According to Goffman, participants in social encounters are similar to actors in an audience. They need to perform to win the audience. Performance requires actors to convey a certain persona that is acceptable and welcoming by the audience. In Goffman's terms, no actor can ever be authentic towards an audience. Blogging, seen as a social action, not face-to-face though, allows the blogger to prepare and present a persona that may be far from the "real" self. A persona that one can rehearse and rewrite until one gets it right (McQuarrie et al., 2013).

In a more recent work on social comparison blogging, is characterised a calculative act (Choi, 2020). The blogger often does not know who their audience is, but very meticulously constructs their identity through their posts (Choi, 2020). Research suggests that identity created on social media, does not necessarily reveal true identity, but rather a desirable identity, which is a yearned identity (Choi, 2016). Bloggers promote their creative-self by working on photo shooting, styling, hair and makeup to achieve "the perfect photo" that will gain them acceptance and recognition in their fashion circle (Choi, 2016). Schau and Gilly (2003) in their study on self-representation on the Web, argue that the web gives the opportunity to plan, refine and rebuild one's self-representation.

The blogger must then show some kind of authoritative leadership. Beverland and Farrelly (2010) in their study on authenticity and authoritativeness within subcultures found that individuals who desired social outcomes engaged in authoritative performance. Authoritative performance in a community requires a self-act rather than a collective act (Arnould & Price, 2003). The authoritative leader makes decisions and expects others to implement them without question (Sadler, 2003). The blogger must establish the authority of her/his taste (McQuarrie et al., 2013).

A fashion leader is an individual with an ability to convince others to accept a new fashion or style (Kim & Hong, 2011). As opposed to fashion followers who tend to be driven by affective processing when presented with new information, are less involved with fashion and spend less time searching for sources to collate information, fashion leaders are driven by both cognitive and affective abilities to work with information, are willing to take risks, seek positive utilitarian and hedonic shopping experiences, have high interest in fashion, high levels of innovativeness and opinion leadership (Lee & Xu, 2022).

5 Blog Development Journey

5.1 *From Personal Blog to Professional Webpage*

Many well-known fashion bloggers including Chiara Ferragni have started their blogging career as hobbyists recording interesting outfits on their blog, using their blog as an online journal for personal disclosure and not as an opportunity to display taste. Posts in this case are usually casual, lack focus, motivation and attention to detail. Soon the blog starts to take the form of a private social media page for friends and family. At the next stage, the blog starts to transit towards a public display of taste. The blogger starts to elaborate on their statements sharing more about their personal taste, style, places they shop, comments over their shopping experience.

At the next stage, a blogger is ready to take risks, and exercise, taste as a power of judgement. It is through these ground-breaking taste displays that the blogger succeeds in being accepted as fashionable and accumulates cultural capital. Good judgement is not enough though. Any catalogue picture will have stylish nice-looking clothes. Fashion is not a matter of write or wrong based on fixed rules. Fashion is not a dress code (Bayley, 1991; Gronow, 1997). To be considered a taste leader, a blogger must go beyond the confounds of established styles and selections of clothing. To be received as a taste leader, a blogger must take risks, create and promote, their own aesthetically pleasing and discriminating taste judgements (McQuarrie et al., 2013).

To maintain good and trusting relationships with their followers, a blogger must demonstrate a high level of credibility. Credibility can be gained through demonstrating knowledge, competency and reference (Mainolfi & Vergura, 2022). Credibility can be maintained by providing greater transparency and being more selective with the editorial content and partnership choices (Mainolfi & Vergura, 2022). A number of studies have found a positive impact of a blogger's credibility on intention to buy

(Esteban-Santos et al., 2018; Hollebeek, 2013; Magno, 2017; Mainolfi & Vergura, 2022).

5.2 From Virtual Community to Audience Management

As bloggers start to share moments from their personal life, the blogger is thrilled to receive comments and interact with the followers. The blog adopts a community feeling. At the second stage, a blogger still eager to please will ask their followers what they would like to see on the blog and will provide as much personal information as they can in order to build a bond with the followers and appear transparent and human. Mathwick et al. (2007) characterise these discussion forums as sites for accumulation of social capital. The blog is managed, perceived as a discussion forum from which all can benefit from exchanging information about fashion clothing and can also participate creating content. The blogger is nothing more than an active participant. At the next stage and as the blogger starts to take risks and promote more of one's personal style and as audience grows larger, the blogger's behaviour changes (McQuarrie et al., 2013). The blogger stops interacting with the audience, stops asking for suggestions, or replying to comments. As the blogger gains independence from the audience, the blogger is considered to be more worthy of an audience (McQuarrie et al., 2013). In the audience belong those consumers who are looking for fashion guidance and they are looking to get this from the blogger who has the taste resource and the leadership characteristics (McQuarrie et al., 2013).

6 Strategies for Maintaining and Growing an Audience

"Once a blogger gains a mass audience and enjoys access to the fashion system, they are no longer an ordinary consumer" (McQuarrie et al., 2013, p. 151).

Research has highlighted two main strategies that bloggers use to build rapport with large audiences: feigning similarity and self-deprecation. Bloggers who have won their audience and have gained access to the fashion industry, although no longer ordinary consumers, often feign similarity with their followers by referring to mundane everyday moments that the followers can relate to while, at the same time, downplaying the special privileges and glamour of life as a fashion insider (McQuarrie et al., 2013).

Self-deprecation is a frequently used strategy. The blogger may critique their own physical characteristics and refer to their own bad habits and embarrassing moments so they appear to be an ordinary consumer, only luckier (McQuarrie et al., 2013). Feigning similarity and self-deprecation strategies create the illusion that a consumer could easily change places with a blogger at any time. It is this misunderstanding of the boundaries on the part of the followers that maintains the audience (McQuarrie et al., 2013). More recent studies on influencer homophily have also found support for the positive effect on consumer information adoption and purchase intention (Bu et al., 2022; Shoenberger & Kim, 2022).

Bloggers seek to expand the influence of their work by the continual addition of new subject matter from their personal lives. The distinction between personal and professional lives becomes increasingly blurred. Brydges and Sjöholm (2019), who studied female personal style bloggers, found that they are unlikely to take a day off even when they are sick and record all the stages from their personal lives including pregnancy and motherhood.

Another technique that fashion bloggers use is tagging, to link information across social media networks. This allows them to present on different platforms simultaneously, attracting more attention and more followers (Bowen & Bowen, 2021).

6.1 From Organising, Styling to Modelling

A blogger may start by putting outfits together using a mood board design software or an outfit maker app. This is usually a safe and cost-effective method that allows the blogger to experiment with different styles and probe and monitor followers' reactions to them (McQuarrie et al., 2013). Bloggers may share pictures from brand websites and fashion shows to create a wish list and make comments on the latest fashions (McQuarrie et al., 2013).

6.2 Building Professional Skills

Professional photography skills are imperative to support the passage from curating to modelling. Taking high-quality photos is seen as a logical consequence of a commitment to higher standards. The blogger can now go beyond the "model in a setting" image to the "less ordinary" image that often appears in upmarket fashion magazines (McQuarrie et al., 2013). A blogger's ongoing commitment to enhancing one's cultural capital is demonstrated through the increasing sophistication of their displays of taste (McQuarrie et al., 2013). This evolution of aesthetic taste is shaped through the interaction with an audience including readers, sponsors and the wider blogger community (Brydges & Sjöholm, 2019).

7 Entrepreneurial Mindset

Management literature and entrepreneurial scholars have taken a keen interest on identifying the personal characteristics, skills and motivations of an entrepreneur when compared to a non-entrepreneur (Bowen & Hisrich, 1986; Busenitz & Barney, 1997; Mitchell et al., 2002). The reason for this is that entrepreneurial characteristics are critical to the success of the entrepreneurial process and the entrepreneurial project ahead (Ibidunni et al., 2020). Although no universal consensus has been reached on the essential characteristics of an entrepreneur (Xie et al., 2021); for the purpose of this study an entrepreneur is defined as a creative, innovative person, risk-taking person who is capable of identifying opportunities in its external environment, use resources in the best way to exploit these opportunities (Cuomo et al., 2017). Other definitions on niece aspects of entrepreneurship such as accidental entrepreneurship, user entrepreneurship, include the commercialisation of a new product and/or service by a group or individuals who are also users of that service/product and highlight the collective nature of the user's entrepreneurial process (Shah & Tripsas, 2007).

Gürol and Atsan (2006) in their study among university students argued that entrepreneurial characteristics are a combination of individual, social and environmental factors. Individual factors or traits include personal characteristics and values; social factors include their family, own background and career stage, while environmental factors are extrinsic characteristics and look at contextual factors such as level of prosperity, tax reductions, timing of opportunities in the career process and socio-cultural constraints to social upheaval and market conditions. Using the trait modelentrepreneurship, Gürol and Atsan (2006) found that students with an inclination for entrepreneurship are more innovative, have more incentives for success, more inner control and more tendency to take risks when compared with students with no inclination for entrepreneurship.

In the context of tourism vlogger entrepreneurs, Xie et al. (2021) found that entrepreneurial vloggers characteristics, sociability, leadership, planning and innovation all have a positive impact on entrepreneurial intentions and performance. Most important were found to be leadership and innovation, but planning also lead entrepreneurs to being better performing individuals. Planning however, was found to have an insignificant effect on entrepreneurial intentions of vloggers, as most vlogging videos in Indian where the study was conducted are unplanned. The study also found that in the early stages, sociability may not have a positive effect because friends are likely to make fun of the vlogger until the last becomes successful and reputable.

In reviewing personal traits of entrepreneurs, the most frequently researched trait among others, are, locus of control, gender identity, risk-taking and the need for achievement (Bowen & Hisrich, 1986). In a recent study on entrepreneurial characteristics among university students, Ibidunni et al. (2020) found support for the positive effect of risk tolerance and need for achievement on entrepreneurial intentions (i.e., identification of business opportunities, motivation to start a business) and positive, but insignificant effect of locus of control on entrepreneurial intentions i.e., (business plan writing). In a study conducted by DeCarlo and Lyons (1979), female entrepreneurs scored significantly higher than females in general. Studies by DeCarlo and Lyons (1979) and Schwartz (1976) found that female entrepreneurs tend to score higher on "masculine" rather than "feminine" values (i.e., achievement, recognition, independence, leadership). Female entrepreneurs who have strong values for achievement and recognition are also expected to seek growth for their business (Bowen & Hisrich, 1986).

Brydges and Sjöholm (2019) highlight the importance of both "soft" and technical skills and argue that both "soft" skills (i.e., communication, organisation, problem solving, decisiveness, leadership) and technical skills to maintain a blog, develop through time and bloggers gain new skills and levels of proficiency through practice (Brydges & Sjöholm, 2019). Entrepreneurial skills are observed to develop through everyday activities, passion derived from hobbies or the need to solve a personal issue may lead to other forms of accidental entrepreneurship (Cuomo et al., 2017). Fitzsimmons and Douglas (2011) distinguishes between four types of entrepreneurs, the accidental entrepreneur (sufficiently high intention, high perceived feasibility, low perceived desirability), the non-entrepreneur (low intention, low feasibility and low desirability), the natural entrepreneur (very high intention, high perceived feasibility, high perceived desirability) and the inevitable entrepreneur (sufficiently high intention, high desirability, low feasibility). We identify Chiara Ferragni as an accidental entrepreneur according to Fitzsimmons and Douglas (2011) with natural characteristics though, that came to surface when the opportunity arose. The following case study aims to describe the passage from an accidental entrepreneur stage to a natural and successful entrepreneur. The process reveals the strategic decisions, resources and motivations in becoming a successful fashion blogger entrepreneur.

8 The Chiara Ferragni—Case Study

8.1 Overview of Chiara Ferragni's Success

Chiara Ferragni according to Forbes, is the #1 fashion influencer in the world (Forbes, 2022), with such a level of influence that Harvard Business School wrote a case study looking into her success in building a personal brand and turning a blog into a profitable business (Keinan et al., 2015).

At present she is a renowned fashion icon and business woman. In 2009, Ferragni started her career as a fashion blogger launching "The Blonde Salad Blog" with the support of her then boyfriend Ricardo Pozzoli (Keinan et al., 2015). The blog was originally financed through standard advertising, product placement and affiliate programmes (Keinan et al., 2015). As Ferragni's reputation increased in 2011, she decided to build her own fashion brand: the Chiara Ferragni Collection. In 2013, she launched her first shoe collection: a line of $220–$500 which sells in 200 stores in 25 countries worldwide (Strugatz, 2014). Her shoe line was so successful that in 2014, only 30% of the revenue came from The Blonde Salad (advertising or brand collaborations). The remaining 70% came from her footwear line (Strugatz, 2014). The next steps were to include other product categories in its collection.

In 2015, Ferragni branches out into other product categories via a capsule collection to be sold exclusively on chiaraferragnicollection.com, including a backpack, a beanie, a T-shirt and an iPhone case all adorned with the "eye" motif from Ferragni's best-selling shoe style (Strugatz, 2015). In 2015, Ferragni had 3.2 million Instagram followers and was on the cover of international publications from Lucky to Grazia to Vogue to

InStyle and Marie Claire (Strugatz, 2015). Ferragni is a favourite collaborator for top luxury fashion brands, i.e., Christian Dior, Chanel and Louis Vuitton, but also collaborates with brands that may not belong to the fashion industry such as the French high-end pastry retailer Ladurée, but as she says she chooses brands she loves to collaborate with for the "surprise effect", and not necessarily brands that belong to the fashion area (Zargani, 2022b).

In 2017, Chiara Ferragni Collection launched pop-ups and exclusive styles with key retailers, including Level Shoes in Dubai, Luisa Via Roma in Florence, IT Hong Kong, Le Bon Marché in Paris, Saks Fifth Avenue in New York and others (Abel, 2017). Ferragni introduces the see-now, buy-now business model at the launch of her new collection in Milan which increased excitement among her followers. Since 2016, however, her business has been underperforming closing in 2017 with a loss. Ferragni took on President, CEO role at Blonde Salad to fine tune operations, reduce fixed costs and invest more on capsule collections (i.e., exclusive collections, offered over a small period of time, in a small number of pieces) to regain profit (Zargani, 2017).

In 2018, her wedding to the Italian singer Fedez was comparable to the royal wedding of Prince Harry and Megan Markle in terms of media impact value. Her influential friends and audience helped her to generate more than $5.2 million in audience-driven Media Impact Value (Tietjen & Collins, 2018). In 2019, Ferragni launched a documentary about her life celebrating the 10th anniversary since the creation of The Blonde Salad (Saliban, 2019). Ferragni, renowned digital entrepreneur, with 15.9 million followers on Instagram was also invited to join the expert committee for the sixth edition of the LVMH Prize for Young Fashion Designers together with other prominent personalities from fashion media and digital fashion entrepreneurs (Diderich, 2019).

In 2020, Chiara Ferragni signed a number of deals to expand her namesake brand. The first one with the Velmar Spa, controlled by the Aeffe Group to produce and distribute Chiara Ferragni beachwear and underwear collections. She also signed a deal with Italian high-end children's wear brand Monnalisa to design cloths for children under 10 years old. A new licencing agreement was also signed with Swinger International to produce of ready-to-wear, handbags and accessories branded Chiara Ferragni (Zargani, 2020a).

Yet, she is not a mere businesswoman, is a role model, a nation's ambassador. Ferragni who at that time had 22 million followers on

Instagram has been also asked by the former Italian Prime Minister Giuseppe Conte to contribute to the fight against the spread of COVID-19 by influencing younger generations to respect the rules and wear sanitary masks (Zargani, 2022a). Together with her husband Fedez, they launched a GoFundMe campaign through a personal donation of 100,000 euros, aimed at delivering new hospital beds to the intensive care unit of Milan's San Raffaele hospital (Tura, 2020). Through this initiative, they collected more than 4.5 million euros and convinced the platform to pledge 250,000 euros from its commissions to other Italian hospitals (Carerra, 2020). In addition, she donated the proceeds from her most recently developed capsule collection with Oreo to a hospital in Bergamo, Italy. Despite not attending Milan's fashion week during the pandemic, Ferragni also supported Milan Fashion Week and Italian brands by wearing a number of Italian looks for free (Zargani, 2020b).

The couple known as the "Ferragnez", received the prestigious annual Ambrogino d'Oro award, bestowed to express gratitude for the contribution they gave to Milan during the pandemic and in recognition of the charity initiatives they promoted throughout that year, starting from their personal donation of 100,000 euros to create new hospital beds. Inviting their followers to also do their part helped to raise almost 4.5 million euros (Zargani, 2022a).

In 2021, Ferragni signed a deal with Safilo Group to produce and distribute her first eyewear collection. She was then named global ambassador for Swiss watchmaker Hublot, ambassador for Bulgari and GHD while continues to have several advertising deals that range from Pantene to Kering-owned luxury brand Pomellato. Ferragni also joined the board of Italian luxury shoe retailer Tod's. Chiara's knowledge and influence on Generation Y and Z will be extremely valuable to Tod's traditional Italian luxury retailer in gaining market share. Investors rewarded the news and shares closed up 14% on the same day with the announcement (Zargani, 2021). The Tod's Group recorded a significant increase in sales. In 2021, revenues are of 883.8 million euros, up 38.7% on 2020. Sales in the retail channel amounted to 659.4 million euros (up 47%) (Tod's Spa, 2021 annual report). In the third quarter alone, revenues of 224.3 million were 14.6% higher than in the third quarter of 2020 and also higher than in the third quarter of 2019 (D'Ascenzo, 2021). A great achievement this, considering the group's turnover and profit results in recent years (Fig. 1). The Ferragni Effect has in fact enabled a relaunch of the group's brands

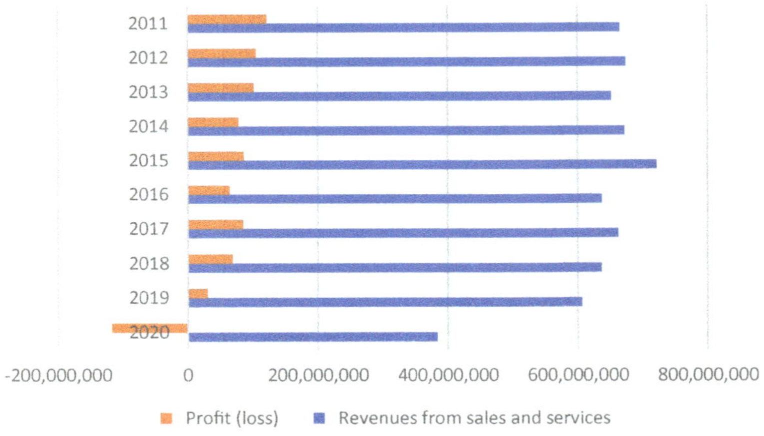

Fig. 1 Tod's Group figures without Ferragni Effect (Euros) (*Source* Authors' elaboration on Bureau Van Dijk data)

(the main ones being Tod's, Hogan, Roger Vivier) especially in the young segment.

In 2021, Ferragni became 100% owner of the TBS Crew that manages The Blonde Salad, the TBS Crew S.L.R closes with sales of 6.8 million euros, climbing 42% on the previous year (Zargani, 2022b). In 2022, her namesake collection has grown to include many different product categories, i.e., accessories, footwear, children's wear, jewellery and other. Her Instagram followers have risen to 27,2 million.

To summarise Chiara Ferragni's entrepreneurial history in Fig. 2, we present a timeline of the main events and business facts.

9 Implications and Recommendations for Fashion Bloggers

We therefore, advise fashion bloggers entrepreneurs to find a unique voice and a distinct style (Delisle & Parmentier, 2016) to stand out from the crowd and inspire others to follow them. To achieve this, it is necessary that bloggers generate cultural and social capital through activities such as visit museums, art exhibitions, watch movies, attend concerts, read books and adopt an active and cosmopolitan lifestyle (i.e.,

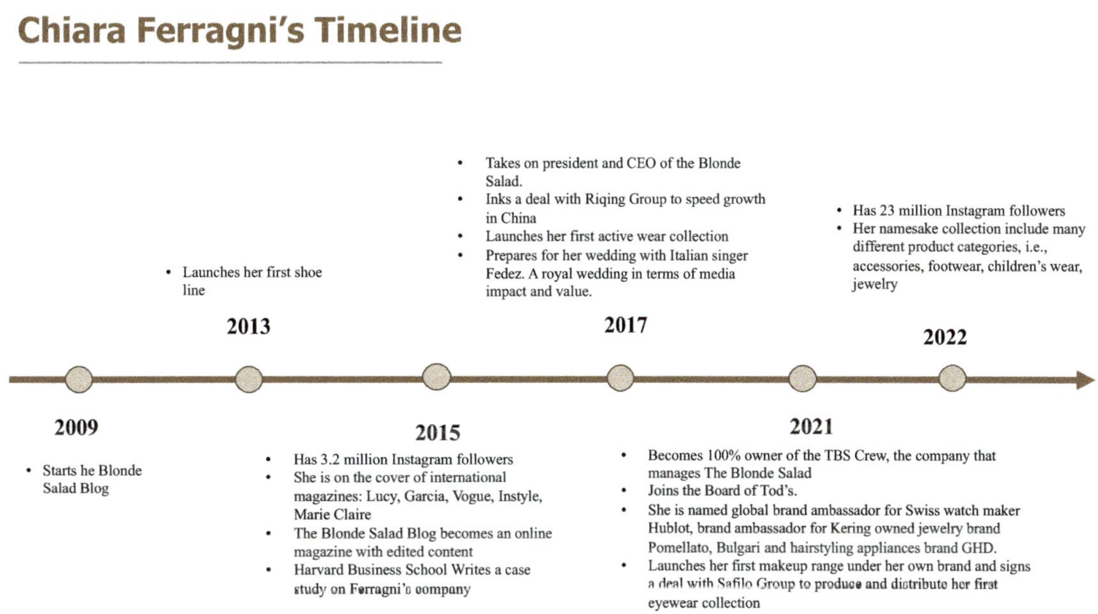

Fig. 2 Chiara's Ferragni Timeline (*Source* Elaborated by the authors based on trade publications and other materials)

attend events, parties and corporate entertainment, Bowen & Bowen, 2021). Essential skills for fashion bloggers also include artistry and business acumen, therefore, taking courses in creative writing, graphic design, styling, understanding trends and trend forecasting, building and managing relationships, building a brand, selling, modelling and photo shooting are skills of primary importance. Complementary skills, include strategic thinking, being able to identify opportunities, select and build collaborations with brands that match the identity of the blog, consider a long-term plan for the blog (i.e., to become a lifestyle magazine), consider offline business activities that can complement the blog (i.e., launch a collection), treat the blog as a business and be concerned with the longevity and monetarisation of the blog. Peripheral skills include, building a support network of peer fashion bloggers and showing sensitivity, awareness to rules, norms and codes of the blogosphere.

10 Conclusion, Research Limitations and Future Research

To conclude and to answer our first question is the blogosphere accessible to ordinary consumers, as Ferragni says: "I think there is space for everyone. The audience decide now; you don't have to pick and choose" (Cochran, 2016). In other words, the entrepreneurial blogosphere is accessible. Yet, a fashion blogger is not an ordinary consumer. "The mere existence of fashion bloggers may disrupt the traditional fashion system, but at the end the fashion blogger can gain a role in the larger fashion system unavailable to an ordinary consumer" (McQuarrie et al., 2013, p. 149). A fashion blog can bring economic, social and cultural benefits to the blogger that are unavailable to ordinary consumers. Economic benefits include gifts, branded merchandising, paid ad placements on the fashion blog, paid sponsorship of blog contests, modelling, branded clothing, accessories and writing for publication. Social benefits include receiving invitations to exclusive parties, runway shows, designer open houses, charity appearances and mentions in the media. The accumulation of cultural benefits that occurs through this interplay of economic and social benefits, thus distance the blogger from the ordinary consumer. The former is elevated at a different stage where he is not only accumulating, but also developing cultural capital through their own meaning, making (styling and curating) and interpretation of fashion (McQuarrie et al., 2013).

What resources ordinary consumers need to become successful entrepreneurs? From Ferragni's case study, it is evident that both extrinsic and intrinsic resources, tangible and intangible, human and financial resources equip a successful entrepreneur. The final question here is what are the key strategic steps in becoming a successful fashion blogger entrepreneur? The answer to this question is, Chiara Ferragni started her blog as a means to express her own personal views on fashion, she wasn't ever scared to take risks, to share her own taste in fashion, she was always very selective in her partnerships with brands, she never accepted money to advertise an outfit she did not agree with, had developed a set of values that were much respected by her followers and business partners, offered a sense of transparency and approachability in her personal life, created a persona that persevered higher principles (i.e., women's empowerment, gender equality, love for the country, etc.). Chiara Ferragni aimed to be more than a mere fashion blogger and her natural entrepreneurial spirit drove her forward almost after each successful collaboration, Ferragni would launch that product category under her namesake brand. In 2022, Chiara Ferragni owns 100% of her business, The TSB Crew Agency, and The Blonde Salad online magazine. Chiara Ferragni also owns the Chiara Ferragni Collection which since 2013 is extended to include a number of product categories within the fashion industry.

Add to that the fact that she and her husband (singer Fedez) have created a nickname that marks them as a brand and as a family. With this nickname, they have become spokespeople for important social causes, have made personal donations and activated fund-raising initiatives for social and health initiatives. We could therefore call her a "visionary" entrepreneur. In addition to having created a profession, that of fashion blogger, practically from scratch, she has evolved it by directing it towards enterprise and socially sustainable entrepreneurship.

This chapter presents a roadmap (Fig. 3) for fashion blogger entrepreneurs starting their career in the fashion industry, demystifies the blog development process, educates fashion bloggers on the skills they need to possess or acquire and presents the opportunities that a well-received fashion blog can bring. It also presents a review of the literature on fashion blogging strategies and the case of the successful fashion blogger entrepreneur Chiara Ferragni. More qualitative research is required to uncover strategies to maintain and grow an audience, acquire social and cultural capital and monetise blogs. Further research is also required to understand the role and potential of fashion blogger entrepreneurs in the metaverse. Brands are spending over $8M more than in 2019 on influencers, much of which will be invested on developing virtual influencers (Chitrakorn, 2021). It would be especially interesting to investigate how avatars can build personalities that are relatable and influential to win the battle for authenticity and trust that is much sought after by today's fashion brands.

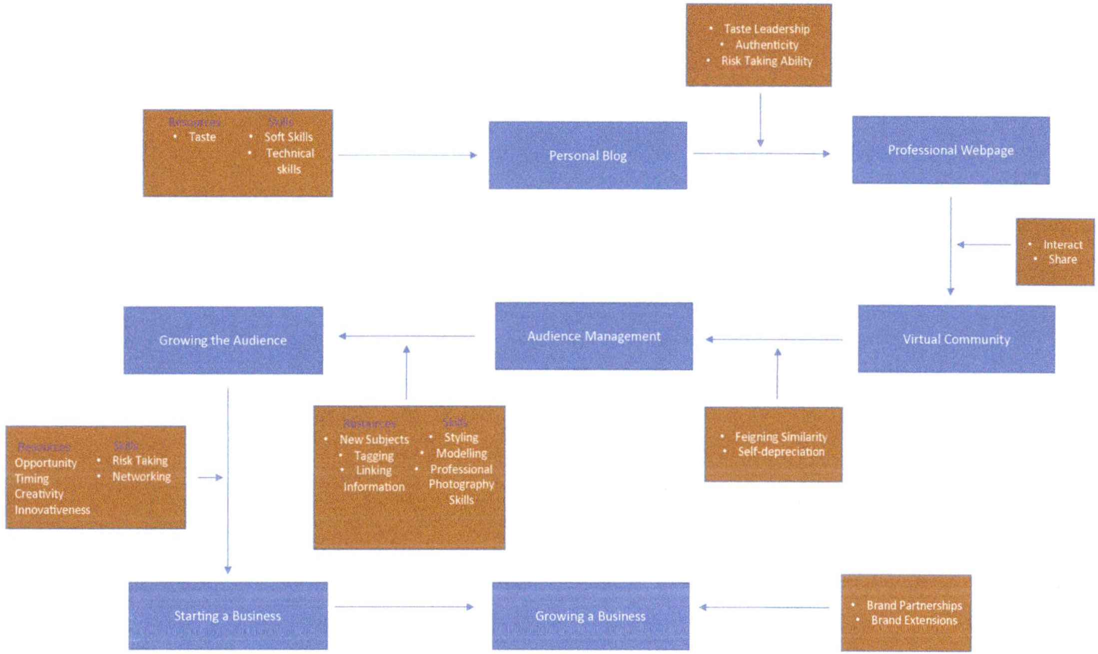

Fig. 3 A theoretical model summarising the necessary and sequential elements to become a fashion blogger entrepreneur (*Source* Developed by the authors based on Bu et al., 2022; McQuarrie et al., 2013; Shoenberger & Kim, 2022)

References

Abel, K. (2017). *Inside Chiara Ferragni's plan for global domination*. Yahoo!life. https://www.yahoo.com/lifestyle/inside-chiara-ferragni-plan-global-185305631.html

Arnould, E. J., & Price, L. L. (2003). Authenticating acts and authoritative performances: Questing for self and community. In S. Ratneshwar, D. G. Mick & C. Huffman (Eds.), *The why of consumption: Contemporary perspectives on consumer motives, goals and desires* (pp. 140–163). Routledge. https://www.routledge.com/The-Why-of-Consumption-Contemporary-Perspectives-on-Consumer-Motives-Goals/Huffman-Mick-Ratneshwar/p/book/9780415316170

Audrezet, A., de Kerviler, G., & Guidry Moulard, J. (2020). Authenticity under threat: When social media influencers need to go beyond self-presentation. *Journal of Business Research, 117*, 557–569. https://doi.org/10.1016/j.jbusres.2018.07.008

Bayley, S. (1991). *Taste: The secret meaning of things*. Pantheon.

Belk, R. W. (1988). *Possession and the extended self*, *15*(September). http://0-web.a.ebscohost.com.serlib0.essex.ac.uk/ehost/pdfviewer/pdfviewer?vid=10&sid=deea865c-442c-4044-ae24-d7a4d44c3de7%40sessionmgr4006

Beverland, M. B., & Farrelly, F. J. (2010). The quest for authenticity in consumption: Consumers' purposive choice of authentic cues to shape experienced outcomes. *Journal of Consumer Research, 36*(5), 838–856. https://doi.org/10.1086/615047

Bowen, G., & Bowen, D. (2021). Fashion bloggers: Temperament and characteristics. In W. Ozuem & S. Ranfagni (Eds.), *The art of digital marketing for fashion and luxury fashion brands*. Palgrave Macmillan. https://doi.org/10.1007/978-3-030-70324-0_4

Bowen, D. D., & Hisrich, R. D. (1986). The female entrepreneur: A career development perspective. *Academy of Management Review, 11*(2), 393–407. https://doi.org/10.5465/amr.1986.4283366

Brydges, T., & Sjöholm, J. (2019). Becoming a personal style blogger: Changing configurations and spatialities of aesthetic labour in the fashion industry. *International Journal of Cultural Studies, 22*(1), 119–139. https://doi.org/10.1177/1367877917752404

Bu, Y., Parkinson, J., & Thaichon, P. (2022). Influencer marketing: Homophily, customer value co-creation behaviour and purchase intention. *Journal of Retailing and Consumer Services, 66*. https://doi.org/10.1016/j.jretconser.2021.102904

Buffolo, M. (2021). *È bastato che l'imprenditrice digitale annunciasse che Safilo produrrà la sua prima linea di occhiali per far balzare di quasi il 12% il titolo della società. E non è la prima volta che accade*. Agenzia

Italia. https://www.agi.it/economia/news/2021-09-14/chiara-ferragni-quanto-vale-impero-13851298/.

Busenitz, L. W., & Barney, J. B. (1997). Differences between entrepreneurs and managers in large organizations: Biases and heuristics in strategic decision-making. *Journal of Business Venturing, 12*(1), 9–30. https://doi.org/10.1016/S0883-9026(96)00003-1

Carerra, M. (2020). Chiara Ferragni on "making the cut", slowing down and the power of social media. *Women's Wear Daily*. https://wwd.com/fashion-news/fashion-features/chiara-ferragni-making-the-cut-social-media-1203557728/

Chitrakorn, K. (2021). *What influencers marketing looks like in the metaverse*. VogueBusiness. https://www.voguebusiness.com/technology/what-influencer-marketing-looks-like-in-the-metaverse

Choi, A. (2016). Fashion photography on social media: Insights from Hong Kong fashion image producers. *International Journal of Management and Applied Research, 3*(4), 130–144. https://doi.org/10.18646/2056.34.16-011

Choi, A. (2020). Social comparison in fashion blogging: "Creative self" as the new genre in fashion communication. *Journal of Fashion Marketing and Management, 24*(4), 651–665. https://doi.org/10.1108/JFMM-07-2019-0140

Cochran, L. (2016). Chiara Ferragni-how a "crazy blogger" turned her life into a shop window. *The Guardian*. https://www.theguardian.com/fashion/2016/nov/29/chiara-farragni-blogger-the-blonde-salad-socia-media-styleposts-multi-million-pound-business

Cuomo, M. T., et al. (2017). Enablers for end-user entrepreneurship: An investigation on Italian food bloggers. *Psychology and Marketing, 34*(12), 1109–1118. https://doi.org/10.1002/mar.21051

D'Ascenzo, M. (2021). *Tod's, Chiara Ferragni entra nel cda e il titolo vola in Borsa*. Finanza. https://www.ilsole24ore.com/art/tod-s-chiara-ferragni-entra-consiglio-amministrazione-ADgnfVWB

DeCarlo, J. F., & Lyons, P. R. (1979). A comparison of selected personal characteristics of minority and nonminority female entrepreneurs. *Proceedings of 39th Annual Meeting of the Academy of Management*, pp. 369–373.

Delisle, M. P., & Parmentier, M. A. (2016). Navigating person-branding in the fashion blogosphere. *Journal of Global Fashion Marketing, 7*(3), 211–224. https://doi.org/10.1080/20932685.2016.1167619

Diderich, J. (2019). Chiara Ferragni to join experts on LVMH prize panel. *Women's Wear Daily*. https://wwd.com/fashion-news/fashion-scoops/chiara-ferragni-to-join-experts-on-lvmh-prize-panel-1202988177/

Duffy, B. E. (2013). Manufacturing authenticity: The rhetoric of "real" in women's magazines. *Communication Review, 16*(3), 132–154. https://doi.org/10.1080/10714421.2013.807110

Esteban-Santos, L., García Medina, I., Carey, L., & Bellido-Pérez, E. (2018). Fashion bloggers: Communication tools for the fashion industry. *Journal of Fashion Marketing and Management, 22*(3), 420–437. https://doi.org/10.1108/JFMM-10-2017-0101

Findlay, R. (2015). The short, passionate, and close-knit history of personal style blogs. *Fashion Theory, 19*(2), 157–178. https://doi.org/10.2752/175174115X14168357992319

Fitzsimmons, J. R., & Douglas, E. J. (2011). Interaction between feasibility and desirability in the formation of entrepreneurial intentions. *Journal of Business Venturing, 26*(4), 431–440. https://doi.org/10.1016/j.jbusvent.2010.01.001

Forbes. (2020). #846b33a4552c. Retrieved January 15, 2022. https://www.forbes.com/top-influencers/fashion/

Goffman, E. (1951). Symbols of class status. *British Journal of Sociology, 2*(4), 294–304. https://doi.org/10.2307/588083

Gronow, J. (1997). *The sociology of taste*. Routledge.

Gürol, Y., & Atsan, N. (2006). Entrepreneurial characteristics amongst university students: Some insights for entrepreneurship education and training in Turkey. *Education + Training, 48*(1), 25–38. https://doi.org/10.1108/00400910610645716

Gustafsson, V., & Khan, M. S. (2017). Monetising blogs: Enterprising behaviour, co-creation of opportunities and social media entrepreneurship. *Journal of Business Venturing Insights, 7*(January), 26–31. https://doi.org/10.1016/j.jbvi.2017.01.002

Hollebeek, L. D. (2013). The customer engagement/value interface: An exploratory investigation. *Australasian Marketing Journal, 21*(1), 17–24. https://doi.org/10.1016/j.ausmj.2012.08.006

Hsieh, L., Child, J., Narooz, R., Elbanna, S., Karmowska, J., Marinova, S., Puthusserry, P., Tsai, T., & Zhang, Y. (2019). A multidimensional perspective of SME internationalization speed: The influence of entrepreneurial characteristics. *International Business Review, 28*(2), 268–283. https://doi.org/10.1016/j.ibusrev.2018.09.004

Ibidunni, A. S., Mozie, D., & Ayeni, A. W. A. A. (2020). Entrepreneurial characteristics amongst university students: Insights for understanding entrepreneurial intentions amongst youths in a developing economy. *Education + Training, 63*(1), 71–84. https://doi.org/10.1108/ET-09-2019-0204

Keinan, A., Maslauskaite, K., Crener, S., & Dessain, V. (2015). *The blonde salad* (pp. 1–25). Harvard Business School.

Kim, H. S., & Hong, H. (2011). Fashion leadership and hedonic shopping motivations of female consumers. *Clothing and Textiles Research Journal, 29*(4), 314–330. https://doi.org/10.1177/0887302X11422819

Klass, M. (2014, September 30). *How fashion blogger makes millions*. Cable News Network. https://edition.cnn.com/videos/international/2014/09/30/spc-fashion-season-chiara-ferragni-blogger.cnn

Lee, H., & Xu, Y. (2022). Influence of motivational orientations on consumers' adoption of virtual fitting rooms (VFRs): Moderating effects of fashion leadership and technology visibility. *International Journal of Fashion Design, Technology and Education, 15*(1), 1–11. https://doi.org/10.1080/17543266.2022.2048423

Mainolfi, G., & Vergura, D. T. (2022). The influence of fashion blogger credibility, engagement and homophily on intentions to buy and e-WOM. Results of a binational study. *Journal of Fashion Marketing and Management, 26*(3), 473–494. https://doi.org/10.1108/JFMM-03-2020-0050

Magno, F. (2017). The influence of cultural blogs on their readers' cultural product choices. *International Journal of Information Management, 37*(3), 142–149. https://doi.org/10.1016/j.ijinfomgt.2017.01.007

Marwick, A. E. (2013). *Status update: Celebrity, publicity, and branding in the social media age*. Yale University Press. http://www.jstor.org/stable/j.ctt5vkzxr

Mathwick, C., Wiertz, C., & de Ruyter, K. (2007). Social capital production in a P3 community. *Journal of Consumer Research, 34*(April), 833–849.

McCracken, G. (1989). Who is the celebrity endorser? Cultural foundations of the endorsement process. *Journal of Consumer Research, 16*(3), 310. https://doi.org/10.1086/209217

McQuarrie, E. F., Miller, J., & Phillips, B. J. (2013). The megaphone effect: Taste and audience in fashion blogging. *Journal of Consumer Research, 40*(1), 136–158. https://doi.org/10.1086/669042

Miller, M. (2015, March 23). *How Chiara Ferragni's blog became an $8 million business* [Video]. CBS. New South. https://www.youtube.com/watch?v=jqebhlBHal8.

Mitchell, R. K., Busenitz, L. W., Lant, T., McDougall, P. P, Morse, E. A., & Smith, J. B. (2002). Toward a theory of entrepreneurial cognition: Rethinking the people side of entrepreneurship research. *Entrepreneurship Theory and Practice, 27*(2), 93–104. https://doi.org/10.1111/1540-8520.00001

O'Connor, C. (2017). Forbes Top influencers: Instagram "it" girl Chiara Ferragni on building A fashion empire. *Forbes*, 2017–2019. https://www.forbes.com/sites/clareoconnor/2017/09/26/forbes-top-influencers-instagram-it-girl-chiara-ferragni-on-building-a-fashion-empire/#7a637ddd3001

Parmentier, M.-A., & Fischer, E. (2012). How athletes build their brands. *International Journal of Sport Management and Marketing, 11*, 106–124.

Parmentier, M.-A., Fischer, E., & Reuber, A. R. (2013). Positioning person brands in established organizational fields. *Journal of the Academy of Marketing Science, 41*(3), 373–387. https://doi.org/10.1007/s11747-012-0309-2

Pedroni, M. (2015). 'Stumbling on the heels of my blog': Career, forms of capital, and strategies in the (sub) field of fashion blogging. *Fashion Theory, 19*(2), 179–199. https://doi.org/10.2752/175174115X14168357992355

Sadler, P. (2003). *Leadership* (2nd ed.). Kogan Page.

Saliban, S. (2019). Details on Chiara Ferragni's docufilm revealed. *Women's Wear Daily*. https://wwd.com/fashion-news/fashion-scoops/chiara-ferragni-docufilm-1202942974/

Sanderson, R. (2019). Chiara Ferragni—The Italian influencer who built a global brand. *Financial Times*, pp. 1–13. https://www.ft.com/content/9adce87c-2879-11e9-a5ab-ff8ef2b976c7

Savignac, B.-M., Parmentier, M.-A., & Marcoux, J.-S. (2012). Consumer-bloggers mobilized in marketing campaigns: A study of opinion leaders' authenticity management in a streetwear community. *Consumer Research, 40*, 81–84. http://www.acrwebsite.org/volumes/1011939/volumes/v40/NA-40

Schau, H. J., & Gilly, M. C. (2003). We are what we post? Self-presentation in personal web space. *Journal of Consumer Research, 30*(3), 385–404. https://doi.org/10.1086/378616

Schwartz, E. B. (1976, Winter). Entrepreneurship: A new female frontier. *Journal of Contemporary Business*, 47–76.

Shah, S. K., & Tripsas, M. (2007). The accidental entrepreneur: The emergent and collective process of user entrepreneurship. *Strategic Entrepreneurship Journal, 1*(1–2), 123–140. https://doi.org/10.1002/sej.15

Shen, Z. (2021). A persuasive eWOM model for increasing consumer engagement on social media: Evidence from Irish fashion micro-influencers. *Journal of Research in Interactive Marketing, 15*(2), 181–199. https://doi.org/10.1108/JRIM-10-2019-0161

Shifman, L. (2018). Testimonial rallies and the construction of memetic authenticity. *European Journal of Communication, 33*(2), 172–184. https://doi.org/10.1177/0267323118760320

Shoenberger, H., & Kim, E. (2022). Explaining purchase intent via expressed reasons to follow an influencer, perceived homophily, and perceived authenticity. *International Journal of Advertising, 41*(1), 1–16. https://doi.org/10.1080/02650487.2022.2075636

Sokolova, K., & Kefi, H. (2020). Instagram and YouTube bloggers promote it, why should I buy? How credibility and parasocial interaction influence purchase intentions. *Journal of Retailing and Consumer Services, 53*, 101742. https://doi.org/10.1016/j.jretconser.2019.01.011

Strugatz, R. (2014). The blonde salad's Chiara Ferragni talks fifth anniversary and footwear launch. *Women's Wear Daily*. https://wwd.com/business-news/media/the-blonde-salads-chiara-ferragni-talks-fifth-anniversary-and-footwear-launch-7888047/

Strugatz, R. (2015). The blonde salad at Harvard. *Women's Wear Daily*. https://wwd.com/business-news/media/the-blonde-salad-at-harvard-8172610/

Tietjen, A., & Collins, A. (2018). Digital download: Chiara Ferragni's wedding outperforms ad campaigns. *Women's Wear Daily*. https://wwd.com/business-news/retail/chiara-ferragni-influencer-wedding-outperforms-ad-campaigns-1202784661/

Tod's Spa. (2021). *Annual report*. https://www.todsgroup.com/en/investor-relations/financial-documents

Tura, A. (2020). Chiara Ferragni, fedez raise 3.3. Million euros in fight against coronavirus crisis. *Women's Wear Daily*. https://wwd.com/fashion-news/fashion-scoops/chiara-ferragni-fedez-launch-campaign-to-support-fight-against-coronavirus-crisis-1203534409/

Veale, N. W. (2010). A comparison between collaborative and authoritative leadership styles of special education administrators. *Journal of the American Academy of Special Education Professionals*, 147–156. https://eric.ed.gov/contentdelivery/servlet/ERICServlet?accno=EJ1137054

Xie, Q., Liu, L., Malik, H., Chupradit, S., & Chupradit, P. W (2021). The influence of entrepreneurial characteristics on the performance of tourism vlogger entrepreneurs. *Frontiers in Psychology, 12*(August), 725545. https://doi.org/10.3389/fpsyg.2021.725545

Zargani, L. (2017). Chiara Ferragni takes on president, CEO role in her company. *Women's Wear Daily*. https://wwd.com/business-news/business-features/chiara-ferragni-takes-on-president-ceo-role-in-her-company-11075897/

Zargani, L. (2020a). Aeffe shares climb after Chiara Ferragni agreement. *Women's Wear Daily*. https://wwd.com/business-news/financial/aeffe-shares-climb-after-chiara-ferragni-agreement-1234664173/

Zargani, L. (2020b). Paris, Milan fashion weeks generated EMV totaling 76.3M euros. *Women's Wear Daily*. https://wwd.com/fashion-news/fashion-scoops/paris-milan-fashion-weeks-generated-emv-totaling-76-3m-euros-1234631737/

Zargani, L. (2021). Tod's group appoints Chiara Ferragni Member of the board. *Women's Wear Daily*. https://wwd.com/business-news/human-resources/tods-group-appoints-chiara-ferragni-board-member-1234797394/

Zargani, L. (2022a). Chiara Ferragni on the power of influence and making a difference. *Women's Wear Daily*. https://wwd.com/fashion-news/fashion-features/chiara-ferragni-power-influence-making-difference-1235088604/

Zargani, L. (2022b). Chiara Ferragni eyes selling stake in her company to fuel further growth. *Women's Wear Daily*. https://wwd.com/business-news/business-features/chiara-ferragni-eyes-selling-stake-fuel-further-growth-1235045769/

CHAPTER 7

Crowdfunding Nascent Fashion Brands

Christopher Buckingham

Abstract With increasingly fierce competition and the sheer volume of competing calls on the viewers' attention in crowdfunding, there is an inherent need for fashion brands that wish to remain significant in their market to be heard through an array of media and social channels simultaneously. This problem is not new. Fashion brands have been at the forefront of the fight to be relevant and add value to their customer segments for some time, implementing various degrees of co-creation has been one way to do this.

Building trust and remaining relevant under these market conditions is a form of competitive capital that must be both earned and considered when strategic choices over positioning and perceptions are being taken in the planning process. Co-creation and customer participation can manifest in many forms that can enhance the relationship of a fashion brand with their target audience. These various forms are the focus of this chapter where best practice and empirical observations of a particularly unique segment of fashion are used to demonstrate how

C. Buckingham (✉)
University of Southampton, Southampton, UK
e-mail: C.R.Buckingham@soton.ac.uk

E. Bazaki and V. Wanick (eds.), *Reinventing Fashion Retailing*, Palgrave Studies in Practice: Global Fashion Brand Management ,
https://doi.org/10.1007/978-3-031-11185-3_7

brand interaction in a crowdfunding campaign can add value. Including the shift from co-creation of authentic experiences with the weaponised consumer as participant and co-creator in the authentication of the brand, to one where the entire supply chain is involved in the authentication process and used to position a brand as one that resonates with their consumers by focusing on human well-being, environmental and/or economic sustainability.

Keywords Crowdfunding · Co-creation · Interactivity

1 Introduction

This chapter focuses on particular strategic choices for participation and interactivity by a fashion brand crowdfunding their vision and an enthusiastic audience for a novel fashion accessory product that was successfully crowdfunded via the Kickstarter platform using the reward model (i.e., the crowd received a 'reward' for pecuniary input). Crowdfunding is defined by Rubinton (2011) as "the process of one party financing a project by requesting and receiving small contributions from many parties in exchange for a form of value to those parties". In the Kickstarter context, these many parties represent a loose collection of agents with niche common interest in the visions being presented on the platform.

Within the theme of this book, this chapter makes an important contribution using novel frameworks from Cheung et al. (2021), and Buckingham and Wanick (2021) to view the congruence of participation and engagement embedded in the strategies employed by the applicant Crowdfunder. This chapter contributes a deeper understanding of the use of the digital environment to help persuade the individuals that make up the audience on Kickstarter to take ex ante crowdfunding purchasing action as argued by Kappel (2009). This chapter's research question asks what strategies a nascent fashion brand can adopt in order to navigate crowdfunding their vision. The importance of this contribution is in the knowledge capital (crowdfunding fluency) that nascent fashion brands can gain to navigate a crowdfunding strategy that helps develop participation and engagement in a crowdfunding campaign. Strategically, fashion brands of all sizes face many choices and issues on how to add value to their brand. Agrawal (2018) stated that utilising a crowdfunding campaign may help to ignite a sense of belonging among the crowd as they become engaged with the process of value creation and feel more connected to both brand and the creative team behind that vision.

Utilising empirical observations from a crowdfunding campaign, this chapter draws on the experiences of a small budding enterprise in a unique sector of fashion accessories that has a tribal following on social media. This chapter will attempt to demonstrate how the use of a crowdfunding campaign allowed a deeper set of interactions between the entrepreneur and the crowd. This interaction contributed to the successful outcomes for this campaign. However, it's easy to overlook some of the issues that crowdfunding applicants face when making strategic decisions about their crowdfunding campaigns.

The focus of this chapter is a unique product in the fashion sector that helps address the research question, but the findings can be generalised to the wider fashion industry in that the interactions witnessed are not necessarily unique to this particular campaign nor the cultural product as outcome. They are generalisable across multiple campaigns in multiple sectors. Although we have a unique paradigm in this chapter, these parameters are not fixed to this particular campaign, nor this particular product. Indeed, they could be applied across multiple campaigns and multiple sectors in fashion.

2 Background

The transition to the concept of a co-creative brand is one marked by a distinction in the fundamental use of the web from a one-way communicative tool to a multi-dimensional service provider where the end user (or for fashion brands—their customer) is responsible for the narratives and outcomes produced in this interaction. The result of this shift is what Occhiocupo and Freiss (2013) classed as an enhanced experience for the consumer of fashion. Experiential marketing in fashion is not new and roots can be found in the need to help fashion brands move beyond a passive approach and to a more active marketing dynamic that meets both the consumers appetite for involvement and the brands need to be more dynamic and connected in their relationship with the consumer. The result is a multi-channel communication strategy that is capable of shifting the production and sale of fashion goods from one where communication was viewed as a corporate after service, to one where the relationship is nurtured and sustained by continuous personal interactions between the parties.

This form of customer integration was what Benkler (2006) predicted as becoming a more common form of interaction, indeed we can trace the concept back further to Pine and Gilmore (1998) who were among the first to welcome readers to the concept and epoch of the experiential economy. In our modern era, we can claim that this novel concept has now been embedded and expected by both the producers and the consumers of fashion.

Furthermore, as Simmel (1957) identified, we shouldn't forget that fashion is a paradox, it is unique as it plays to the aspirations and practical needs of the consumer simultaneously, it seeks to imitate and to be novel at once and on occasions, even more paradoxically, to the same market. The paradox continues with Yan et al. (2015) as the novelty that is sought can be expressed as a renewal of itself (bringing back past designs) and the creation of spaces to exchange and update existing personal inventory with pre-owned products from a previous age. The result is a consistent objective within the fashion sector to be innovative within the confines of the consumer's demands and perceived trends. This results in constant evolution of the product and differentiation from previous iterations of inventory.

Relationships are formed out of respect for this novelty and co-creation, Thomas et al. (2020) saw this as the confluence where the value that results from these forms of interaction are now themselves motivating factors for the consumer's involvement. This has now become an axiom for the modern brand where social media has allowed for Benklers (2006) predictions to become somewhat realised. This is an age characterised for the marketer as one of engagement and value co-creation via the multiple channels that are open and utilised by the stakeholders in this sphere. Fashion brands can enact a form of routine maintenance through engagement with their audiences on social media. Pillot de Chenecey (2019) argues that trust in brands generally has crashed to an all-time low, but the utility of social media is a form of salvation for the concept of the brand. Especially in industries that have been under increasing pressure as media attention has focused on diversity, financial and environmental wrong doings. The world of fashion has not escaped this focus; however, we are also finding examples of brands excelling in their adoption and utilisation of this new mode of communication. In seeking a lens to view how new fashion brands are coming to their market with baked-in strategies that help them navigate this new terrain identified by Bogusky and Windsor (2009), we turn to crowdfunding in this chapter as a way to explore the novelty that is being created by allowing members of the crowd to purchase ex ante novel fashion products and digitally engage with the entrepreneur behind the brand.

3 Crowdfunding

Crowdfunding is an emerging form of marketing that allows nascent brands to communicate the uniqueness in a way that would have not been possible pre-crowdfunding era. Crowdfunding has a long history and some of the most significant cultural works have relied on some form of pecuniary input from diverse people. To cite but one example in literature, and one of the more notable for me, writing this in Winchester, UK, is Jane Austen who used a list system as a form of crediting contribution to her published works. Therefore, when we talk about crowdfunding in this chapter, we are talking about the modern form that utilises the web to convey messages and inspire contributions (in some form) to a specific project.

There are many crowdfunding models but for the purposes of this chapter, we will be focusing on one model, the reward model, where the applicant seeking funding offers the contributing members of the crowd an incentive of some form, normally a product. This has been compared to shopping where members of the crowd are 'buying' earlier than the general public outside of the campaign or crowdfunding platform are able to access. The unique aspect of this is that the applicant and their associated branding are using the communicative aspect of the crowdfunding strategy to help shape the perceptions of the funder. This is not restricted to the platform as we shall see, social media, external to the platform, plays a major role in this process of engagement. For the crowdfunding platform, this may be a risky proposition in that they have lost control over the communications that happen between the applicant and the crowd essential to the creation and then distribution of the campaign they host on their platform.

For the Funder too this may be problematic, Jane Austen's literature remains in circulation and reprints are commissioned but the list of the original contributors to help that product become a reality are not equally published with each run of reprints. These names would have no relevance or value for the majority of the readership today, and the same loss is conferred on the Crowdfunder of fashion. The Funders, as Rouzé (2019), highlights, are forgotten but the product remains. Those who helped to create the fashion product are lost in the temporal ether and in some ways no longer matter, as the product is out there on the market, for a majority of the public, which individuals in a society funded the vision, is of little concern.

In terms of the producers themselves, it may be more significant in the narrative that emerges, especially if the creators decide at some future point to make a further attempt at creating and distributing a product utilising crowdfunding. The point here is that the crowd are agents in their own right and beyond the social kudos of being able to brag about their contribution to the creation of the brand, or the enterprise, their agency is lost in the entrepreneurial marketing of the brand itself. Stokes (2000) argued for entrepreneurial marketing to be positioned as an innovative concept that at its heart has a focus on value creation from the bottom-up, led by marketing methods which are interactive by nature.

Borrowing from Kappel (2009), we can think of the reward model of crowdfunding as a post-ante transaction that is primarily leading to cultural consumption of a cultural product that in this instance is a fashion output. Crowdfunding can thus be seen as part of the cultural production leading to cultural outputs. Through this lens, we can see that fashion products, part of the creative sector, are embedded in a business model where the concept of risk is transferred from the pre-crowdfunding model of production first and marketing second, to a new normative business strategy that both sidesteps traditional financial intermediaries and shifts the greater part of the risk in this production to the members of the crowd. As Rouzé (2019) identifies, this allows for better alignment between the desires of the crowd and the applicant to create products that have far greater forms of personalisation and offer creators an outlet to markets that may have otherwise been more difficult to penetrate. The result is a more diversified set of cultural products that are more readily matched to a more diverse, niche audience. As Pillot de Chenecey (2019) points out, niche in this respect doesn't mean small, a global niche may contain significant numbers.

Positioning crowdfunding as a means of communication results in a view of the concept as a new form of communicative capital that adds to our understanding from the perspective of cultural production. Pre-crowdfunding, production followed predicted trends and the concept of mass production followed the business model that allowed scale (and at times scope) to produce higher margins for the producer and to some degree allowed the producer to influence consumption and taste. This only presents part of the picture for production which also followed consumption in a tussle with consumers that saw fashion brands trying to stay on trend. Helped by electronic points of sale technology, fashion brands in this epoch were able to meet the demands of an ever-changing customer base. The persona of the customer could be better matched with the outcome and just in time, production techniques were applied in the fashion industry. Braham (1997) highlighted ways in which producers and retailers attempted to stay more relevant and more on target as they concentrated their efforts on ever narrower consumer groups.

Fast forward to an age where the power of the consumer is in their codified voice, and a time when they are willing to express these vocalised experiences with the products and the brands, and we arrive at a very different place. This contemporary era is a further defining moment where established brands seek engagement with their target audience through the use of common associations. In this approach, the audience are given thematic topics which are fed to them from the marketing side of the corporate body in order to aid the identification of common characteristics of the brands audience. Dialogue is the intended outcome as their audience meet and greet and para-socialise via common interests centred around the brand. This is what Godey et al. (2016) termed the profile-based connectivity strategy. The strategy is centred around the creation of moments where the audience organically respond to the conditioning that has been designed around the core information deposits that engage the audience and provoke dialogue.

A further strategy, particularly relevant here, is also identified by Godey et al. (2016), that of the content-based strategy In this strategy, the brand is more aligned to a production company seeking to entertain an audience rather than merely engage them via commonality. Here, the brand goes much further in producing content that entertains and in so doing attempts to create an emotional response from their audiences. The problem in this strategy is that the emotional outcome may not be positive, in which case careful management of the potential for a backlash against the brand is needed.

Note the change in lexicon from that of the consumer to that of the audience. The emphasis of shifting to the concept of the value being created as a co-created outcome. The IPC stakeholder map from Buckingham and Wanick (2021) is particularly relevant in this pattern of behaviour and especially when the fashion brand utilises crowdsourcing or crowdfunding to engage an audience. The Investor, Producer, Consumer

(IPC) Stakeholder map outlines the main contribution to a campaign as one of three characteristics: as an investor, as a producer or as a consumer. The crowdfunding model allows a member of the crowd to be one of these agents or a combination of two or all three at one time. This is not unique to crowdfunding, as was highlighted by Legge and Hindle (2004), Business Angels and some Venture Capitalists have long been recognised for their multifaceted contributions to entrepreneurial projects. In the crowdfunding context, it has been recognised by Beier and Wagner (2014) and Vismara (2018), that a shift has taken place in that the professional advisor and investor has given way to a more amateur stakeholder who none-the-less has the possibility to add value for the relationship (Fig. 1).

Building and maintaining relationships with the consumer tribe base is paramount in building a successful brand. If crowdfunding is the chosen route for the nascent brand to start funding communications about their entrepreneurial journey, then relationship building and exchanges via social media are at the forefront of this strategy, and they need to have begun prior to the live stages of a campaign. The effort the parties

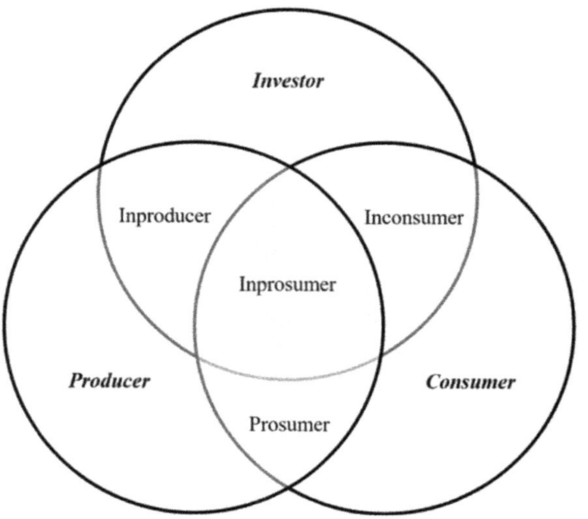

Fig. 1 The IPC Stakeholder Map (Buckingham & Wanick, 2021). Produced with permission of the copyright owner

contribute to the relationship has a direct impact on the quality of the interactions that follow, as witnessed by Cheung et al. (2021).

For this chapter, we chose a unique and under-researched genre of fashion as the lens, that of the badge or pin. A small item that can be manufactured relatively cheaply and one not demanding a large production base to make it affordable to many in the consumer market. Small designs are the key which are often creatively associated with a particular identity. This genre of fashion was also chosen as the distance between creator and customer are closely aligned, creators often interact directly with community members via social media channels beyond the crowdfunding campaign. The extent to which this helps to build a niche brand can be seen in the way these nascent brands convey a sense of independence from corporate environments, even though they consistently make use of corporate platforms to make and retain relationships with their consumer tribe base. Cheung et al. (2021) identified five connected elements in their research for Social Media Marketing (SMM) activities where engagement and interactivity between parties can be established.

Utilising the framework from Cheung et al. (2021), enables this chapter to map the types of interactivities and engagement that campaigns are able to produce on the Kickstarter platform and beyond on other (Etsy, Instagram, Patreon and Twitter) digital channels. The messages on Kickstarter were from four independent members of the crowd who were all treated to responses from the applicant. Three of these four were 'superbackers' which in Kickstarter parlance means they have contributed to 25 campaigns in the previous 12 months. As such, it can be inferred that these backers had greater levels of confidence in the use of the Kickstarter platform and so may feel they have a greater expectation in terms of response from the applicant, which in turn, may have influenced the applicant to produce a more rapid response.

Combining these frameworks may provide greater insights but without detailed research being conducted with ethics approval, there are limitations in defining exactly who belonged to more than one category in the IPC map. This lack of insight results in the view of the investor (backer), producer (creating their own products for funding via Kickstarter) or consumer (purchasing the product) being indistinct. This is an issue for any Kickstarter campaign that is being viewed *externally*—the investor is also a consumer and the investment is not just about funding, it can also be focused on sharing the campaign with their network as well as being associated with a purchasing action. Furthermore, the Cheung et al.

(2021) framework lacks insight for the actions that are required from the brand owners. There may be sensitivities that concern intellectual property, the business model being adapted/adopted or in any other issue that means detailed information being conveyed to an anonymous third party via the crowdfunding campaign may need to be considered as this may constitute disclosing sensitive information that could be advantageous to competitors (Table. 1).

Extending the implicit features of this taxonomy further, we can see that the Business of Fashion (BoF) (2019) playbook on influencer strategy develops the concept with four types of influencers which in turn relate to the strategic objective of the brand which they align with an influencer type. This type is based solely on the size of the influencer's follower network, which ranges from nano (1k–10k followers), micro (10k–100k), mid (100k–500k) and macro (500k+). The message is explicit in the playbook, ensuring that the brand is aligned with the right type (i.e., size) of influencer before any activity is pursued.

This adds a further layer to the considerations of brand management when deciding on the operationalised strategic objectives of the participation that they wish to engage in with their customers. The level of engagement and participation can be measured against the five social media marketing elements from Cheung et al. (2021) and the level of

Table 1 The five social media marketing elements from Cheung et al. (2021)

Heading	*Criteria*
Entertainment	Releasing the unlocked capital that creates a sense of happiness and pleasure among the crowd. It requires the brand owners to be a little playful in their approach
Customisation	Being able to add extra items and track the pledges that had been made and receiving insider details. For the brand owner this requires a strategy of being responsive to customers
Interactivity	Consumers discuss brand stories and offer personal insights to the community. For brand owners this also entails direct discussions with their consumers
eWoM	Credible and trustworthy distribution of past experiences of personal interactions with the brand. Linked closely with interactivity, this can be initiated by past, present or future customers
Trendiness	Timely, insightful and fashionable updates on the brands social media channels. Updates tend to send quality signals and help to retain interactions among the cohort who follow them

influencer engagement as classified by BoF (2019). But that is dependent on the use of influencers in the campaign. There was no evidence that influencers had been targeted in the case study below. Furthermore, budgetary constraints could be a barrier for many smaller brands in utilising this form of advertising.

This also raises a question of authenticity, if influencers were themselves to become aware of these brands and the products they are producing, then this is an organic find on behalf of the influencers, making this a more authentic communication with their audiences. The alternative is a transactional agreement between the influencer and the brand, the fact they have aligned themselves with the brand and the product is in itself a recognition that the influencer has some shared values that have resulted in them discussing and sharing (at some level) the product and brand with their audience.

4 Case Study

Kickstater: https://www.kickstarter.com/projects/bluelyboo/witches-enamel-pin-collection/posts/3260714
Web Site: https://bluelyboo.com/
BluelyBoo was an overfunded project realised by 285 backers who contributed £10,242 at the end of July 2021 to the campaign that had a target raise of £300. The project was for a set of enamel pins (badges) which were themed around witchcraft. These handmade pins were of varied colour and size but were between 40mm for the larger ones and 20mm for the mini pins, which were made available to purchase once £4200 had been pledged. In Kickstarter parlance, this is known as 'unlocking' a reward where a certain pledge level acts as an incentive to encourage the crowd to pledge further funding to gain access to these new levels of product.

Beyond the Kickstarter campaign, which ran from 6th July to 17th August 2021, BluelyBoo were also present on Etsy, Instagram, Patreon (subscriptions) and Twitter. There were three ranges offered by the brand: fashion accessories, pins (the focus of the crowdfunding campaign) and stationary. All products were distinctive and followed the same themes of colourful stylised representations of real and imaginary animals, artefacts and people.

In terms of the business strategy employed, BluelyBoo overachieved in their crowdfunding endeavour and were innovative in their approach

Fig. 2 Collection of enamel pins from the BluelyBoo Kickstarter campaign (reproduced with the copyright owner's permission)

to the market with a subscription plan available from their site. With this subscription plan, the consumer received a new pin every month. The subscription service was promoted at various touch points by the brand and was actively promoted by the consumers via eWoM (electronic word of mouth) (Fig. 2).

As with many Kickstarter projects, the branding was embedded with the project and although there was no significant or obvious branding in the campaign itself, the external sites did have more salient and explicit branding. The communication aspect of the campaign was also well-balanced in terms of the five SMM elements identified by Cheung et al. (2021). These elements were: entertainment, customisation, interactivity, eWoM and trendiness.

The brand consistently engaged with each of the five categories as demonstrated in Table 2 below where the activities they conducted are mapped.

5 Recommendations

Future research may find it possible to combine the IPC Stakeholder map from Buckingham and Wanick (2021) with the framework proposed by Cheung et al. (2021). In doing so, future researchers will be able to better demonstrate not just the use of the elements for engagement and

Table 2 Mapping BluelyBoo's activities

Heading	*Action*
Entertainment	The applicant was responsive to the customer's questions and input in the campaigns comments sections. This included external social media channels (Twitter, Instagram). The tone was light but professional and the responses centred only on the products
Customisation	BluelyBoo were responsive to the pecuniary input from the crowd unlocking various rewards as the values increased and encouraging these incremental offers with dialogue that directly addressed the audience and highlighted the perceived value that could be gained
Interactivity	Across social media channels, BluelyBoo was more active than on the Kickstarter pages. This may reflect the social capital gained by the audience and the need for the applicant to be responsive to the audience on their terms (where permission is granted to talk directly to the audience). Evidence for this is found in the interaction and dialogue that both parties engaged in
eWoM	This connects with interactivity, in that the permissions granted are for the dialogue to be open and engaging, but also able to deliver some quality in the signals being transmitted and received and in the levels of pleasure received by the parties in this process. If this experience turns into a negative one, then the pleasurable aspects of the interactions are diminished. This does not appear to be the situation in this case as dialogue continued in the campaign
Trendiness	Use of a monthly subscription service as a novel approach to the engagement of the audience and consistent appeal with a commitment to deliver by the brand via the Patreon platform

interaction in the crowdfunding campaign strategy but also show who was participating by highlighting the identity and level of those involved. Doing so may add to the theoretical understanding of the agents that combine to make up the crowd and their motivation for taking action. The space in this chapter did not allow the author an opportunity to empirically study this element, but it would present future researchers with an impactful project that may have practical consequences as the levels of digital engagement can be mapped against these criteria.

For practitioners, the framework that could emerge from this exploration could be a useful way to determine if their campaign will be fit for purpose. By using the combined frameworks, practitioners in the fashion ecosystem may find it beneficial to utilise this as a checklist for their activities and strategic planning process prior to launching a campaign. In doing so, more robust and better planned crowdfunding campaigns may result.

Not all crowdfunding campaigns are born equal. Some have large budgets that enable the campaign to develop graphics, text or more polished video and thus the size of a campaign and budgetary constraints could affect the type of campaign that future researchers use as their lens. The various categories that exist within the category of fashion also result in a wide range of cultural products being produced. This may be of interest to future researchers, where the differences between products as outcomes and the campaigns that accompany these products, can be better understood. There is a dearth of research on the impact on cultural outputs this type of constraint may yield within the crowdfunding context.

6 Conclusion

This short chapter has focused on the digital engagement of a small fashion brand and highlighted the recent shift in communication strategies to one where the communicative aspect of the brand is always 'on' and allows consumer permission to engage with the brand. This shift is thus one that moves from a corporate culture of communication as an after-service function to one where it becomes a necessary strategy spanning multiple channels.

Positioning crowdfunding as a fresh strategic approach to communications for nascent brands, it becomes less focused on the funding element and more on the crowd, thus crowdfunding is a form of marketing and communicative activities that has a levelling effect by being open to smaller, nascent fashion businesses. By engaging with the process of crowdfunding, these new businesses also gain additional capital via the fluency they gain in learning about the planning and implementing processes involved in a crowdfunding campaign. This allows this chapter to address the research question on strategies a nascent fashion brand can adopt in order to navigate crowdfunding their vision.

For the agents that make up the crowd, they may be forgotten in time, but their legacy continues as the products and brands they help create gain traction in the market. This is part of the process where entrepreneurial marketing is baked-in for a bottom-up value creation process. This creates a better fit between the needs and desires of the individuals that form to make up the crowd and the final products that emerge. More responsive and engaged dialogue lend themselves to the discovery of products that are more aligned to niche markets. Crowdfunding thus becomes a new form of communicative capital where profile-based or content-based strategies are employed by the brand in their communications planning.

For future research, understanding the identity of the agents in the crowd through the IPC mapping exercise and the SMM five-step framework, deeper insights into the identities and the strategies being utilised can be gained. These insights would add value for the literature on both fashion and crowdfunding. A start in this direction was made in this chapter as we thinly explored a campaign using the SMM five-step framework. This demonstrated how interaction and engagement were used in a successful campaign. For future researchers, thicker insights will be gained, best practice could be highlighted with implications for both theory and practice.

References

Agrawal, A. J. (2018). 12 Key strategies to a successful crowdfunding campaign. *Entrepreneur Europe*. https://www.entrepreneur.com/article/307250.

Beier, M., & Wagner, K. (2014). Crowdfunding between social media and e-commerce: Online communication, online relationships and fundraising success on crowdfunding platforms. *Swiss Institute for Entrepreneuship*, http://papers.ssrn.com/sol3/papers.cfm?abstract_id=2512470.

Benkler, Y. (2006). *The wealth of networks: How social production transforms markets & freedom*, Yale University Press.

Bogusky, A. & Windsor, J. (2009). *Baked in: Creating products and businesses that market themselves*. B2 Books.

Braham, P. (1997). Fashion: Unpacking a cultural production In Paul Du Gay (ed.), *Cultures of production, productions of culture*. Sage.

Buckingham, C. & Wanick, V. (2021). Crowdfunding serious games: Toward a framework In Fabio Perez Marzullo & Felipe Antonio de Oliveira (Eds.), *Practical perspectives on educational theory & game development*, pp. 112–129. IGI Global.

Business of Fashion. (2019). *How to maximise your influencer strategy*. Business of Fashion Limited.

Cheung, M. L., Pires, G., Rosenberger, P. J, III., Leung, W. K. S., & Chang, M. K. (2021). *The Role of Social Media Elements in Driving Co-Creation and Engagement. Asia Pacific Journal of Marketing and Logistics*. https://doi.org/10.1108/APJML-03-2020-0176

Godey, B., Manthiou, A., Pederzoli, D., Rokka, J., Aiello, G., Donvito, R., & Singh, R. (2016). Social media marketing efforts of luxury brands: Influence on brand equity and consumer behavior. *Journal of Business Research., 69*(12), 5833–5841.

Kappel, T. (2009). Ex ante crowdfunding and the recording industry: A model for the U.S.? *Loyola of Los Angeles Entertainment Law Review., 29*, 375–385.

Legg, J., & Hindle, K. (2004). *Entrepreneurship: Context, vision & planning*. Palgrave Macmillan.

Occhiocupo, N., & Friess, M. (2013). Exploring what motivates consumers to co-create value in virtual fashion communities In Proceedings of *the Naples forum on service*. 1–16. Naples, Italy. http://www.naplesforumonservice.it/uploads/files/Occhiocupo,%20Friess.pdf

Pillot de Chenecey, S. (2019). *The post-truth business: How to rebuild brand authenticity in a distrusting world*. Kogan Page.

Pine II, J. B., & Gilmore, J. H. (1998). Welcome to the experience economy. *Harvard Business Review*. July—August. 97–105.

Rouze, V. (2019). Far from an alternative: Intermediation apparatuses, In Vincent Rouze (ed.). *Cultural crowdfunding: Platform capitalism, labour & globalization*. University of Westminster Press.

Rubinton, J. B. (2011). Crowdfunding: Disintermediate investment banking. *Social Science Research Network*. https://papers.ssrn.com/sol3/papers.cfm?abstract_id=1807204

Simmel, G. (1957). Fashion. *American Journal of Sociology.*, *62*(6), 541–558.

Stokes, D. (2000). Putting entrepreneurship into marketing: The processes of entrepreneurial marketing. *Journal of Research in Marketing and Entrepreneurship.*, *2*(1), 1–16.

Thomas, L. J., Brooks, S., & McGouran, C. (2020). Antecedents of value co-creation activities for online fashion brands. *Journal of Strategic Marketing.*, *28*(5), 384–398.

Vismara, S. (2018). Information cascades among investors in equity crowdfunding. *Entrepreneurship, Theory & Practice.*, *42*(3), 467–497.

Yan, R., Bae, S. Y., & Xu, H. (2015). Second-hand clothing shopping among college students: The role of psychographic characteristics. *Young Consumers.*, *16*(1), 85–98.

Index

E. Bazaki and V. Wanick (eds.), *Reinventing Fashion Retailing*, Palgrave Studies in Practice: Global Fashion Brand Management,
https://doi.org/10.1007/978-3-031-11185-3

GPSR Compliance
The European Union's (EU) General Product Safety Regulation (GPSR) is a set of rules that requires consumer products to be safe and our obligations to ensure this.

If you have any concerns about our products, you can contact us on

ProductSafety@springernature.com

In case Publisher is established outside the EU, the EU authorized representative is:

Springer Nature Customer Service Center GmbH
Europaplatz 3
69115 Heidelberg, Germany

www.ingramcontent.com/pod-product-compliance
Ingram Content Group UK Ltd.
Pitfield, Milton Keynes, MK11 3LW, UK
UKHW022222051026
15624UKWH00002B/307
* 9 7 8 3 0 3 1 1 1 1 8 4 6 *